PANDEMIC OBSESSION

'Let no man seek
Henceforth to be foretold what shall befall
Him or his children.'

From John Milton's *Paradise Lost* XI, 770–72 and inscribed on the title page of Mary Shelley's *The Last Man* (1826)

PANDEMIC OBSESSION

HOW THEY FEATURE IN OUR POPULAR CULTURE

AN ANTHOLOGY OF HISTORICAL WRITING, FINE ART, POEMS AND POPULAR LITERATURE

COMPILED BY STEPHEN BASDEO

AN IMPRINT OF PEN & SWORD BOOKS LTD.
YORKSHIRE – PHILADELPHIA

First published in Great Britain in 2023 by
PEN AND SWORD HISTORY
An imprint of
Pen & Sword Books Ltd
Yorkshire – Philadelphia

ISBN 978 1 39909 221 0

A CIP catalogue record for this book is available from the British Library.

Typeset in Times New Roman 12/16 by
SJmagic DESIGN SERVICES, India.
Printed and bound in the UK by CPI Group (UK) Ltd.

Pen & Sword Books Limited incorporates the imprints of Atlas, Archaeology, Aviation, Discovery, Family History, Fiction, History, Maritime, Military, Military Classics, Politics, Select, Transport, True Crime, Air World, Frontline Publishing, Leo Cooper, Remember When, Seaforth Publishing, The Praetorian Press, Wharncliffe Local History, Wharncliffe Transport, Wharncliffe True Crime and White Owl.

For a complete list of Pen & Sword titles please contact
PEN & SWORD BOOKS LIMITED
47 Church Street, Barnsley, South Yorkshire, S70 2AS, England
E-mail: enquiries@pen-and-sword.co.uk
Website: www.pen-and-sword.co.uk

Or
PEN AND SWORD BOOKS
1950 Lawrence Rd, Havertown, PA 19083, USA
E-mail: Uspen-and-sword@casematepublishers.com
Website: www.penandswordbooks.com

Contents

Introduction

pandemic
noun
/pæn'dem·ɪk/
a dangerous disease that infects many people at one time

When the swine flu (H1N1) pandemic hit the UK in 2009, I was working part-time for the NHS Direct telephone advice service as a non-clinical health advisor. The job itself was fairly simple: I was the first point of contact for people who thought they had symptoms of the disease – which, for many people, were virtually indistinguishable from a range of other illnesses – and to log the details of their call ready for a nurse to call them back. In normal times, the NHS Direct job was fairly easy – a call handler would get at least 10 minutes between calls. This was not so during the swine flu pandemic; calls were taken pretty much back to back. Then, as we all know, the pandemic soon subsided. The swine flu calls to NHS Direct became less frequent. The government had stockpiled Tamiflu for patients which, in turn, eased pressure on the health service. My job became easier.

Of course, less than a decade later, the world would face another pandemic. Rumours of a virus coming out of Wuhan, China, began to circulate in the news. The authoritarian Chinese government, so it was rumoured, actually imprisoned some Wuhan residents into their homes in order to contain the virus. The measures that the Chinese government resorted to did not work. The virus soon found its way into the subcontinent, Europe and the Americas.

When the coronavirus/Covid-19 pandemic struck the UK in 2020, I confess that I was quite optimistic and I assumed it would be just like the swine flu: a few chaotic months for the NHS after which we could all breathe again. Then came the talk of social distancing around April and May. 'We didn't have to do that during swine flu,' I remarked to a family member as we were watching the news. Then a lockdown was announced during which all non-essential businesses were forced to close and many employees were placed on furlough. The news channels beamed horrifying pictures of Italian hospitals that had been overwhelmed with Covid-19 patients. As I write this in November 2021, the death toll in the UK stands at somewhere around 140,000. I was clearly wrong: Covid-19 was nothing at all like the swine flu pandemic. Currently, the UK does have a glimmer of hope in the country's vaccine programme and, at the time of writing, over 40 million people have received two doses.

Even at this point we find that Covid-19 has made a mark on our popular culture. Several academics have written commentaries on Covid-19 in publications like the *Conversation*, the *Guardian*, and the *London Review of Books*. Several medieval scholars seeking to enhance their own blogs and their niche research interests have drawn parallels between the days of Covid-19 and the fourteenth-century Black Death – some of these comparative essays have, shall we say, stretched some of those historical analogies. At the time of writing, I see that new history books on pandemics are beginning to appear in publishers' online catalogues. The poets have not been silent either – slowly trickling forth from several publishers' presses are new anthologies of poems focusing on life in lockdown. I have also noticed anthologies of short stories based around the theme of living during a pandemic. I shall be bold and make a prediction that, before 2022 is finished, full-length pandemic and post-apocalyptic novels will be published en masse. The recent surge of history books looking at past pandemics cannot fail to have been noticed by anyone with even a passing interest in history (indeed, some might say my own book is part of this trend). Films have already started to appear: Michael Bay's *Songbird* (2020) was a big-budget depiction of the world a few years hence when Covid-19 has mutated into Covid-23 and the populace is kept in a state of permanent lockdown. The movie *Contagion* (2011) likewise enjoyed a resurgence in popularity on streaming platforms such as Amazon Prime and Netflix. At the lower end of the scale is a film such as the gloriously bad *Coronazombies* (2020).

The annals of history are littered with accounts of pandemics and these pandemics have, in turn, shaped human culture. One of the earliest large-scale pandemics to have affected Ancient Greece and the Middle East was the so-called Athenian Plague. What we in the modern age call Ancient Greece was not actually a single, unified country but a collection of independent city states; the five most important – in terms of military power and wealth – were Athens, Sparta, Corinth, Thebes and Delphi. As well as facing threats from hostile neighbouring powers such as Persia, relationships between the Ancient Greek city states (*poleis*) were by no means peaceful and, at various points, conflicts would break out as one state vied for supremacy over the others. The Peloponnesian War (431–4 BC) was one such internecine conflict. It was a war between the Delian League, led by Athens – a significant naval power – and the Spartan-led Peloponnesian League – which had a powerful land army. The Athenian historian Thucydides (460–c.400 BC), a member of the Athenian aristocracy, wrote a history of this war, *The History of the Peloponnesian War* which, as the title implies, gave a chronological account of the events of the conflict. Thucydides' history has some claim to being the first 'scientific' history book written – the Ancient Greek gods have no active role in the events recounted, which is in stark contrast to earlier histories written by Herodotus. As Thucydides said, his work was *not* a romance but a serious scholarly inquiry which would serve as a resource for future ages.[1] Thucydides also strove to be impartial in his writing – a practice followed as much as possible by modern historians – despite being an Athenian himself.

For our purposes, Thucydides' history is most notable because it contains an account of the Athenian Plague, to which event he was an eyewitness. Athens was a port city and one of the main trading hubs in the Mediterranean; even in the ancient world, news travelled fast and, in the first year of the war, reports filtered through to Athens of a deadly plague which had first raised its head in Ethiopia, and had then appeared in Egypt and Libya, before the disease itself finally reached Athens. There is no way of definitively knowing what the plague was and whatever it was originally has likely evolved over the course of twenty-five centuries;[2] various candidates for the Athenian Plague include bubonic plague, typhus, smallpox and measles. The most probable among those listed, however, was typhus.[3] Most people believed that diseases were spread by miasma: foul air infected your body. However, Thucydides, who was ahead of his time, posited the concept of contagion.[4] He believed that infected people directly passed the disease on to others – just how it was spread, however, Thucydides was not quite sure. If a person caught it, then it usually killed them within a week and those who survived it suffered blindness, memory loss, and even the loss of their limbs. Any treatment that relied on the theory of the four humours – in which, to be healthy, the body had to maintain an equilibrium of blood, yellow bile, black bile and phlegm – was sure to be largely ineffective, and as Thucydides remarked, 'No remedy was found that could be used as a specific; for what did good in one case, did harm in another.'[5]

The ravages of the plague caused the decline of the Athenian Empire, just as pandemics have been responsible for the downfall or fundamental restructuring of other societies in different times. Thucydides was one of the first in a long line of historians, chroniclers, poets, and later, novelists and filmmakers, to represent pandemics in literature. This book, then, focuses more specifically on plague and is an anthology of sources that gives readers a glimpse into how several plague pandemics throughout history have left their mark in religious writings, history books, poetry, popular fiction and fine art (included in the plates with captions).

Stephen Basdeo
December 2021

Bubonic Plague

Plague, or *Yersinia pestis*, has 'plagued' humankind throughout history. Since at least the reign of Byzantine Emperor Justinian in the 500s – and likely for much longer before that – it has claimed millions of lives. This section presents the voices of people throughout history who have recorded their experiences of the plague and who have also represented it in popular culture.

The Possible First Appearance of Bubonic Plague in History

The first example, from the Old Testament or Tanakh, needs very little introduction. A key religious text in both the Jewish and Christian religions, it tells the story of the creation of the world; the early history of the Jewish people – including their escape from Egyptian slavery, their wars and conquests throughout the Middle East, and the establishment of an Israelite kingdom – as well as outlining the laws under which they lived. The Tanakh is best viewed as a combination of both history and mythology; leaving aside debates about the veracity of some of the events recorded in the Tanakh, one particular passage is noteworthy for the book of Samuel appears to give us the first appearance of the bubonic plague. Completed by 550 BC, the Book of Samuel tells of a war between the Israelites and the Philistines, as well as, in the later chapters, the rise of the united Kingdom of Israel under King David. In this passage, the Philistines, having defeated the Israelites in battle, capture the Ark of the Covenant and carry it back to the temple of their heathen god Dagon. Soon the Philistines are afflicted with a plague; the presence of rodents in this passage and the appearance of boils on the skin strongly suggest that the plague in question is bubonic.[6]

From The Old Testament, 1 Samuel 5:10-12; 6 (King James Version)

Chapter 5

Therefore they sent the ark of God to Ekron. And it came to pass, as the ark of God came to Ekron, that the Ekronites cried out, saying, They have brought about the ark of the God of Israel to us, to slay us and our people.

So they sent and gathered together all the lords of the Philistines, and said, Send away the ark of the God of Israel, and let it go again to his own place, that it slay us not, and our people: for there was a deadly destruction throughout all the city; the hand of God was very heavy there.

And the men that died not were smitten with the emerods: and the cry of the city went up to heaven.

Chapter 6

And the ark of the LORD was in the country of the Philistines seven months.

And the Philistines called for the priests and the diviners, saying, What shall we do to the ark of the LORD? tell us wherewith we shall send it to his place.

And they said, If ye send away the ark of the God of Israel, send it not empty; but in any wise return him a trespass offering: then ye shall be healed, and it shall be known to you why his hand is not removed from you.

Then said they, What shall be the trespass offering which we shall return to him? They answered, Five golden emerods, and five golden mice, according to the number of the lords of the Philistines: for one plague was on you all, and on your lords.

Wherefore ye shall make images of your emerods, and images of your mice that mar the land; and ye shall give glory unto the God of Israel: peradventure he will lighten his hand from off you, and from off your gods, and from off your land.

Wherefore then do ye harden your hearts, as the Egyptians and Pharaoh hardened their hearts? when he had wrought wonderfully among them, did they not let the people go, and they departed?

Now therefore make a new cart, and take two milch kine, on which there hath come no yoke, and tie the kine to the cart, and bring their calves home from them:

And take the ark of the LORD, and lay it upon the cart; and put the jewels of gold, which ye return him for a trespass offering, in a coffer by the side thereof; and send it away, that it may go.

And see, if it goeth up by the way of his own coast to Bethshemesh, then he hath done us this great evil: but if not, then we shall know that it is not his hand that smote us: it was a chance that happened to us.

And the men did so; and took two milch kine, and tied them to the cart, and shut up their calves at home:

And they laid the ark of the LORD upon the cart, and the coffer with the mice of gold and the images of their emerods.

And the kine took the straight way to the way of Bethshemesh, and went along the highway, lowing as they went, and turned not aside to the right hand or to the left; and the lords of the Philistines went after them unto the border of Bethshemesh.

And they of Bethshemesh were reaping their wheat harvest in the valley: and they lifted up their eyes, and saw the ark, and rejoiced to see it.

And the cart came into the field of Joshua, a Bethshemite, and stood there, where there was a great stone: and they clave the wood of the cart, and offered the kine a burnt offering unto the LORD.

And the Levites took down the ark of the LORD, and the coffer that was with it, wherein the jewels of gold were, and put them on the great stone: and the men of Bethshemesh offered burnt offerings and sacrificed sacrifices the same day unto the LORD.

And when the five lords of the Philistines had seen it, they returned to Ekron the same day.

And these are the golden emerods which the Philistines returned for a trespass offering unto the LORD; for Ashdod one, for Gaza one, for Askelon one, for Gath one, for Ekron one;

And the golden mice, according to the number of all the cities of the Philistines belonging to the five lords, both of fenced cities, and of country villages, even unto the great stone of Abel, whereon they set down the ark of the LORD: which stone remaineth unto this day in the field of Joshua, the Bethshemite.

And he smote the men of Bethshemesh, because they had looked into the ark of the LORD, even he smote of the people fifty thousand and threescore and ten men: and the people lamented, because the LORD had smitten many of the people with a great slaughter.

And the men of Bethshemesh said, Who is able to stand before this holy LORD God? and to whom shall he go up from us?

And they sent messengers to the inhabitants of Kirjathjearim, saying, The Philistines have brought again the ark of the LORD; come ye down, and fetch it up to you.

The Plague of Justinian; or, the Pestilence that Brought Down an Empire

In 476, the Western Roman Empire fell when the 'barbarian' Odoacer proclaimed himself King of Rome and deposed the last Roman Emperor of the western half of the empire, Romulus Augustulus. Various civil wars, barbarian invasions and diseases in the centuries preceding the end of the empire had contributed to its fall. However, the Eastern Roman, or Byzantine, Empire, with its capital at Constantinople, did not fall in 476. Then, in

527, Justinian ascended the throne of the Eastern Empire and set about reconquering Rome's 'lost' lands in the west. Initially, this strategy went well; Justinian's generals managed to retake Carthage, Rome and Ravenna – the seat of the old Roman emperors – and it seemed as though the Roman Empire might once more be united. Yet it was not to be. In 542, the bubonic plague descended upon the empire and Justinian himself even caught it. Justinian survived but many of his subjects did not. The extract below is an account from Procopius, a member of the Byzantine court, who included a description of the plague in his *History of the Wars of Justinian*.

From *History of the Wars of Justinian* by Procopius (c. AD 550)

[AD 542] During these times there was a pestilence, by which the whole human race came near to being annihilated.[7] Now in the case of all other scourges sent from Heaven some explanation of a cause might be given by daring men, such as the many theories propounded by those who are clever in these matters; for they love to conjure up causes which are absolutely incomprehensible to man, and to fabricate outlandish theories of natural philosophy, knowing well that they are saying nothing sound, but considering it sufficient for them, if they completely deceive by their argument some of those whom they meet and persuade them to their view. But for this calamity it is quite impossible either to express in words or to conceive in thought any explanation, except indeed to refer it to God. For it did not come in a part of the world nor upon certain men, nor did it confine itself to any season of the year, so that from such circumstances it might be possible to find subtle explanations of a cause, but it embraced the entire world, and blighted the lives of all men, though differing from one another in the most marked degree, respecting neither sex nor age. For much as men differ with regard to places in which they live, or in the law of their daily life, or in natural bent, or in active pursuits, or in whatever else man differs from man, in the case of this disease alone the difference availed naught. And it attacked some in the summer season, others in the winter, and still others at the other times of the year. Now let each one express his own judgment concerning the matter, both sophist and astrologer, but as for me, I shall proceed to tell where this disease originated and the manner in which it destroyed men.

It started from the Aegyptians who dwell in Pelusium. Then it divided and moved in one direction towards Alexandria and the rest of Aegypt, and in the other direction it came to Palestine on the borders of Aegypt; and from there it spread over the whole world, always moving forward and travelling at times favourable to it. For it seemed to move by fixed arrangement, and to tarry for a specified time in each country, casting its blight slightingly upon none, but spreading in either direction right out to the ends of the world, as if fearing lest some corner of the earth might escape it. For it left neither island nor cave nor mountain ridge which had human inhabitants; and if it had passed by any land, either not affecting the men there or touching them in indifferent fashion, still at a later time it came back; then those who dwelt round about this land, whom formerly it had afflicted most sorely, it did not touch at all, but it did not remove from the place in question until it had given up its just and proper tale of dead, so as to correspond exactly to the number destroyed at the earlier time among those who dwelt round about. And this disease always took its start from the coast, and from there went up to the interior. And in the second year it reached Byzantium in the middle of spring, where it happened that I was staying at that time. And it came as follows. Apparitions of supernatural beings in human guise of every description were seen by many persons, and those who encountered them thought that they were struck by the man they had met in this or that part of the body, as it happened, and immediately upon seeing this apparition they were seized also by the disease. Now at first those who met these creatures tried to turn them aside by uttering the holiest of names and exorcising them in other ways as well as each one could, but they accomplished absolutely nothing, for even in the sanctuaries where the most of them fled for refuge they were dying constantly. But later on they were unwilling even to give heed to their friends when they called to them, and they shut themselves up in their rooms and pretended that they did not hear, although their doors were being beaten down, fearing, obviously, that he who was calling was one of those demons. But in the case of some the pestilence did not come on in this way, but they saw a vision in a dream and seemed to suffer the very same thing at the hands of the creature who stood over them, or else to hear a voice foretelling to them that they were written down in the number of those who were to die. But with the majority it came about that they were seized by the disease without becoming aware of what was coming either through a waking vision or a dream. And they were taken in the following manner. They had a sudden fever, some when just roused from sleep, others while walking about, and others while otherwise engaged, without any regard to what they were doing. And the body shewed no change from its previous colour, nor was it hot as might be expected when attacked by a fever, nor indeed did any inflammation set in, but the fever was of such a languid sort from its commencement and up till evening that neither to the sick themselves nor to a physician who touched them would it afford any suspicion of danger. It was natural, therefore, that not one of those who had contracted the disease expected to die from it. But on the same day in some cases, in others on the following day, and in the rest not many days later, a bubonic swelling developed; and this took place not only in the particular part of the body which is called 'boubon,' that is, below the abdomen, but also inside the armpit, and in some cases also beside the ears, and at different points on the thighs.

Up to this point, then, everything went in about the same way with all who had taken the disease. But from then on very marked differences developed; and I am unable to say whether the cause of this diversity of symptoms was to be found in the difference in bodies, or in the fact that it followed the wish of Him who brought the disease into the world. For there ensued with some a deep coma, with others a violent delirium, and in either case they suffered the characteristic symptoms of the disease. For those who were under the spell of the coma forgot all those who were familiar to them and seemed to be sleeping constantly. And if anyone cared for them, they would eat without waking, but some also were neglected, and these would die directly through lack of sustenance. But those who were seized with delirium suffered from insomnia and were victims of a distorted imagination; for they suspected that men were coming upon them to destroy them, and they would become excited and rush off in flight, crying out at the top of their voices. And those who were attending them were in a state of constant exhaustion and had a most difficult time of it throughout. For this reason everybody pitied them no less than the sufferers, not because they were threatened by the pestilence in going near it (for neither physicians nor other persons were found to contract this malady through contact with the sick or with the dead, for many who were constantly engaged either in burying or in attending those in no way connected with them held out in the performance of this service beyond all expectation, while with many others the disease came on without warning and they died straightway); but they pitied them because of the great hardships which they were undergoing. For when the patients fell from their beds and lay rolling upon the floor, they kept patting them back in place, and when they were struggling to rush headlong out of their houses, they would force them back by shoving and pulling against them. And when water chanced to be near, they wished to fall into it, not so much because of a desire for drink (for the most of them rushed into the sea), but the cause was to be found chiefly in the diseased state of their minds. They had also great difficulty in the matter of eating, for they could not easily take food. And many perished through lack of any man to care for them, for they were either overcome by hunger, or threw themselves down from a height. And in those cases where neither coma nor delirium came on, the bubonic swelling became mortified and the sufferer, no longer able to endure the pain, died. And one would suppose that in all cases the same thing would have been true, but since they were not at all in their senses, some were quite unable to feel the pain; for owing to the troubled condition of their minds they lost all sense of feeling.

Now some of the physicians who were at a loss because the symptoms were not understood, supposing that the disease centred in the bubonic swellings, decided to investigate the bodies of the dead. And upon opening some of the swellings, they found a strange sort of carbuncle that had grown inside them.

Death came in some cases immediately, in others after many days; and with some the body broke out with black pustules about as large as a lentil and these did not survive even one day, but all succumbed immediately. With many also a vomiting of blood ensued without visible cause and straightway brought death. Moreover I am able to declare this, that the most illustrious physicians predicted that many would die, who unexpectedly escaped entirely from suffering shortly afterwards, and that they declared that many would be saved, who were destined to be carried off almost immediately. So it was that in this disease there was no cause which came within the province of human reasoning; for in all cases the issue tended to be something unaccountable. For example, while some were helped by bathing, others were harmed in no less degree. And of those who received no care many died, but others, contrary to reason, were saved. And again, methods of treatment shewed different results with different patients. Indeed the whole matter may be stated thus, that no device was discovered by man to save himself, so that either by taking precautions he should not suffer, or that when the malady had assailed him he should get the better of it; but suffering came without warning and recovery was due to no external cause.

And in the case of women who were pregnant death could be certainly foreseen if they were taken with the disease. For some died through miscarriage, but others perished immediately at the time of birth with the infants they bore. However, they say that three women in confinement survived though their children perished, and that one woman died at the very time of child-birth but that the child was born and survived.

Now in those cases where the swelling rose to an unusual size and a discharge of pus had set in, it came about that they escaped from the disease and survived, for clearly the acute condition of the carbuncle had found relief in this direction, and this proved to be in general an indication of returning health; but in cases where the swelling preserved its former appearance there ensued those troubles which I have just mentioned. And with some of them it came about that the thigh was withered, in which case, though the swelling was there, it did not develop the least suppuration. With others who survived the tongue did not remain unaffected, and they lived on either lisping or speaking incoherently and with difficulty…

Now the disease in Byzantium ran a course of four months, and its greatest virulence lasted about three. And at first the deaths were a little more than the normal, then the mortality rose still higher, and afterwards the tale of dead reached five thousand each day, and again it even came to ten thousand and still more than that. Now in the beginning each man attended to the burial of the dead of his own house, and these they threw even into the tombs of others, either escaping detection or using violence; but afterwards confusion and disorder everywhere became complete. For slaves remained destitute of masters, and men who in former times were very prosperous were deprived of the service of their domestics who were either sick or dead, and many houses became completely destitute of human inhabitants. For this reason it came about that some of the notable men of the city because of the universal destitution remained unburied for many days.

And it fell to the lot of the emperor, as was natural, to make provision for the trouble. He therefore detailed soldiers from the palace and distributed money, commanding Theodorus to take charge of this work; this man held the position of announcer of imperial messages, always announcing to the emperor the petitions of his clients, and declaring to them in turn whatever his wish was. In the Latin tongue the Romans designate this office by the term 'referendarius.' So those who had not as yet fallen into complete destitution in their domestic affairs attended individually to the burial of those connected with them. But Theodorus, by giving out the emperor's money and by making further expenditures from his own purse, kept burying the bodies which were not cared for. And when it came about that all the tombs which had existed previously were filled with the dead, then they dug up all the places about the city one after the other, laid the dead there, each one as he could, and departed; but later on those who were making these trenches, no longer able to keep up with the number of the dying, mounted the towers of the fortifications in Sycae, and tearing off the roofs threw the bodies in there in complete disorder; and they piled them up just as each one happened to fall, and filled practically all the towers with corpses, and then covered them again with their roofs. As a result of this an evil stench pervaded the city and distressed the inhabitants still more, and especially whenever the wind blew fresh from that quarter.

At that time all the customary rites of burial were overlooked. For the dead were not carried out escorted by a procession in the customary manner, nor were the usual chants sung over them, but it was sufficient if one carried on his shoulders the body of one of the dead to the parts of the city which bordered on the sea and flung him down; and there the corpses would be thrown upon skiffs in a heap, to be conveyed wherever it might chance. At that time, too, those of the population who had formerly been members of the factions laid aside their mutual enmity and in common they attended to the burial rites of the dead, and they carried with their own hands the bodies of those who were no connections of theirs and buried them. Nay, more, those who in times past used to take delight in devoting themselves to pursuits both shameful and base, shook off the unrighteousness of their daily lives and practised the duties of religion with diligence, not so much because they had learned wisdom at last nor because they had become all of a sudden lovers of virtue, as it were – for when qualities have become fixed in men by nature or by the training of a long period of time, it is impossible for them to lay them aside thus lightly, except, indeed, some divine influence for good has breathed upon them – but then all, so to speak, being thoroughly terrified by the things which were happening, and supposing that they would die immediately, did, as was natural, learn respectability for a season by sheer necessity. Therefore as soon as they were rid of the disease and were saved, and already supposed that they were in security, since the curse had moved on to other peoples, then they turned sharply about and reverted once more to their baseness of heart, and now, more than before, they make a display of the inconsistency of their conduct, altogether surpassing themselves in villainy and in lawlessness of every sort. For one could insist emphatically without falsehood that this disease, whether by chance or by some providence, chose out with exactitude the worst men and let them go free. But these things were displayed to the world in later times.

During that time it seemed no easy thing to see any man in the streets of Byzantium, but all who had the good fortune to be in health were sitting in their houses, either attending the sick or mourning the dead. And if one did succeed in meeting a man going out, he was carrying one of the dead. And work of every description ceased, and all the trades were abandoned by the artisans, and all other work as well, such as each had in hand. Indeed in a city which was simply abounding in all good things starvation almost absolute was running riot. Certainly it seemed a difficult and very notable thing to have a sufficiency of bread or of anything else; so that with some of the sick it appeared that the end of life came about sooner than it should have come by reason of the lack of the necessities of life. And, to put all in a word, it was not possible to see a single man in Byzantium clad in the chlamys, and especially when the emperor became ill (for he too had a swelling of the groin), but in a city which held dominion over the whole Roman empire every man was wearing clothes befitting private station and remaining quietly at home. Such was the course of the pestilence in the Roman Empire at large as well as in Byzantium. And it fell also upon the land of the Persians and visited all the other barbarians besides.

The Plague of AD 664: The First Pandemic in English History

The Plague of AD 664 is the first recorded pandemic in English history. It was accompanied with strange signs in the heavens. As the *Anglo-Saxon Chronicle* tells us: 'This year the sun was eclipsed, on the eleventh of May; and Erkenbert, King of Kent, having died, Egbert his son succeeded to the kingdom … there was a great plague in the island Britain.'[8] For their knowledge of this plague, often called 'The Yellow Plague,'[9] historians are mostly reliant on ecclesiastical writings such as those by Bede – whose remarks on the plague are featured below – and most sources do not go into depth regarding patients' symptoms; instead the plague is usually presented as a part of a larger divine plan or punishment. After all, had not Jesus told his followers to expect pestilences during the end times? The plague could not have come at a worse time for the Anglo-Saxon people, who had experienced a century of internecine warfare and invasions from across the sea[10] and, in some cases, this plague made people abandon their faith in God.[11] Along with Saint Bede's account below is an extract from John of Fordun's *Chronicle of the Scottish Nation* which, although written much later, in the fourteenth century, proves that despite the lack of contemporary sources, the Plague of AD 664 was never forgotten.

The View from England from *Ecclesiastical History of England* by Saint Bede (c. AD 731)

In the same year of our Lord 664, there happened an eclipse of the sun, on the third day of May, about the tenth hour of the day.[12] In the same year, a sudden pestilence depopulated first the southern parts of Britain, and afterwards attacking the province of the Northumbrians, ravaged the country far and near, and destroyed a great multitude of men. By this plague the aforesaid priest of the Lord, Tuda, was carried off, and was honourably buried in the monastery called Paegnalaech. Moreover, this plague prevailed no less disastrously in the island of Ireland. Many of the nobility, and of the lower ranks of the English nation, were there at that time, who, in the days of the Bishops Finan and Colman, forsaking their native island, retired thither, either for the sake of sacred studies, or of a more ascetic life; and some of them presently devoted themselves faithfully to a monastic life, others chose rather to apply themselves to study, going about from one master's cell to another. The Scots willingly received them all, and took care to supply them with daily food without cost, as also to furnish them with books for their studies, and teaching free of charge.

The View from Scotland from *Chronicle of the Scottish Nation* by John of Fordun (14th century)

Now after the death of Ferchardus, Maldewinus, son of King Donaldus, attained the throne of the kingdom, in AD 664, the twenty-first year of the emperor Constantine.[13] In that year, Saint Colman returned to Scotland, and was succeeded by Tuda. But, throughout the whole time that the Scots preached in England, unshaken peace and communion prevailed, without the din of strife. At length, when the Anglic clergy of native extraction had increased and multiplied, chiefly through the teaching of the Scots, they all ungratefully began to turn against their holy teachers, and to seek frequent and sundry opportunities of forcing them to return to Scotland, or bear the intolerable burden which was laid upon them. Hence, thereafter, for the twenty years that Maldwynus reigned, there seldom, if ever, happened to be peace between the kingdoms; but, on either side, outbreak followed upon outbreak, with almost ceaseless devastation.

Nevertheless, no battle worthy of mention is found in the chronicles of either nation, to have been fought during this time. But in the fifth year of this king, the whole of Europe was laid low by the horrible calamity of a most grievous death-sickness among men. Adomnan, making mention of this calamity, says: – It is by no means meet to pass over in silence the death-sickness which, in our time, twice wasted the greater part of the earth. For – not to speak of the other more extensive countries of Europe, Italy to wit, and the city of Rome itself, the Cisalpine provinces of Gaul, and the Spaniards, who are shut off by the barrier of the Pyrenean mountains, the islands of the ocean, Ireland and Britain, to wit, were twice utterly devastated by this cruel pestilence; with the exception of two nations, namely, the Scots and the Picts, divided from one another by the mountains of the backbone of Britain (Drumalban) between them. And though neither of these nations are free from great sins whereby the Eternal Judge is oftentimes provoked to wrath, nevertheless He has hitherto patiently borne with them in His mercy, and spared them both.

The Black Death

The Black Death was one of the worst pandemics in history. Originating in China in 1338, the plague spread across Europe, Asia and North Africa, and is estimated to have killed over a third of the European population. Mass graves were a common sight and many people thought that this was a sign of the end times. The plague died down in around 1353 but periodic outbreaks persisted over the next century.

This extract is from Henry Knighton's *Chronicle*; Knighton, who died in 1396, recorded the arrival of the plague in England.

The Black Death Comes to England: From *Knighton's Chronicle* by Henry Knighton (c.1378–1396)

The grievous plague penetrated the seacoasts from Southampton, and came to Bristol, and there almost the whole strength of the town died, struck as it were by sudden death.[14] There died at Leicester in the small parish of St. Leonard more than 380, in the parish of Holy Cross more than 400; in the parish of S. Margaret of Leicester more than 700; and so in each parish a great number. Then the bishop of Lincoln gave general power to all and every priest to hear confessions, and absolve with full and entire authority except in matters of debt, in which case the dying man, if he could, should pay the debt while he lived, or others should certainly fulfil that duty from his property after his death. In the same year there was a great plague of sheep everywhere in the realm so that in one place there died in one pasturage more than 5,000 sheep, and so rotted that neither beast nor bird would touch them. And there were small prices for everything on account of the fear of death. For there were very few who cared about riches or anything else... Sheep and cattle went wandering over fields and through crops, and there was no one to go and drive or gather them for there was such a lack of servants that no one knew what he ought to do. Wherefore many crops perished in the fields for want of someone to gather them. The Scots, hearing of the cruel pestilence of the English, believed it had come to them from the avenging hand of God, and – as it was commonly reported in England – took their oath when they wanted to swear, 'By the foul death of England.

Meanwhile the king sent proclamation that reapers and other labourers should not take more than they had been accustomed to take (in pay). But the labourers were so lifted up and obstinate that they would not listen to the king's command, but if anyone wished to have them he had to give them what they wanted, and either lose his fruit and crops, or satisfy the wishes of the workmen.

After the pestilence, many buildings, great and small, fell into ruins in every city for lack of inhabitants, likewise many villages and hamlets became desolate, not a house being left in them, all having died who dwelt there; and it was probable that many such villages would never be inhabited. In the winter following there was such a want of servants in work of all kinds, that one would scarcely believe that in times past there had been such a lack. And so all necessities became so much dearer.

Giovanni Boccaccio was an Italian writer who composed the *Decameron* between 1348 and 1353, when the Black Death in Europe was at its height. It is a work of fiction, being a collection of ten tales told, as the framing narrative, or 'proem,' suggests, by a group of ten Florentines who have decided to flee to the countryside to escape the Black Death in Florence.

The Black Death in Florence: 'Proem' from *Decameron* by Giovanni Boccaccio (c.1349–1353)

As often, most gracious ladies,[15] as I bethink me, how compassionate you are by nature one and all, I do not disguise from myself that the present work must seem to you to have but a heavy and distressful prelude, in that it bears upon its very front what must needs revive the sorrowful memory of the late mortal pestilence, the course whereof was grievous not merely to eye-witnesses but to all who in any other wise had cognisance of it…

I say, then, that the years of the beatific incarnation of the Son of God had reached the tale of one thousand three hundred and forty-eight when in the illustrious city of Florence, the fairest of all the cities of Italy, there made its appearance that deadly pestilence, which, whether disseminated by the influence of the celestial bodies, or sent upon us mortals by God in His just wrath by way of retribution for our iniquities, had had its origin some years before in the East, whence, after destroying an innumerable multitude of living beings, it had propagated itself without respite from place to place, and so, calamitously, had spread into the West.

In Florence, despite all that human wisdom and forethought could devise to avert it, as the cleansing of the city from many impurities by officials appointed for the purpose, the refusal of entrance to all sick folk, and the adoption of many precautions for the preservation of health; despite also humble supplications addressed to God, and often repeated both in public procession and otherwise, by the devout; towards the beginning of the spring of the said year the doleful effects of the pestilence began to be horribly apparent by symptoms that shewed as if miraculous.

Not such were they as in the East, where an issue of blood from the nose was a manifest sign of inevitable death; but in men and women alike it first betrayed itself by the emergence of certain tumours in the groin or the armpits, some of which grew as large as a common apple, others as an egg, some more, some less, which the common folk called gavoccioli. From the two said parts of the body this deadly gavocciolo soon began to propagate and spread itself in all directions indifferently; after which the form of the malady began to change, black spots or livid making their appearance in many cases on the arm or the thigh or elsewhere, now few and large, now minute and numerous. And as the gavocciolo had been and still was an infallible token of approaching death, such also were these spots on whomsoever they shewed themselves. Which maladies seemed to set entirely at naught both the art of the physician and the virtues of physic; indeed, whether it was that the disorder was of a nature to defy such treatment, or that the physicians were at fault – besides the qualified there was now a multitude both of men and of women who practised without having received the slightest tincture of medical science – and, being in ignorance of its source, failed to apply the proper remedies; in either case, not merely were those that recovered few, but almost all within three days from the appearance of the said symptoms, sooner or later, died, and in most cases without any fever or other attendant malady.

Moreover, the virulence of the pest was the greater by reason that intercourse was apt to convey it from the sick to the whole, just as fire devours things dry or greasy when they are brought close to it. Nay, the evil went yet further, for not merely by speech or association with the sick was the malady communicated to the healthy with consequent peril of common death; but any that touched the cloth of the sick or aught else that had been touched or used by them, seemed thereby to contract the disease.

So marvellous sounds that which I have now to relate, that, had not many, and I among them, observed it with their own eyes, I had hardly dared to credit it, much less to set it down in writing, though I had had it from the lips of a credible witness.

I say, then, that such was the energy of the contagion of the said pestilence, that it was not merely propagated from man to man but, what is much more startling, it was frequently observed, that things which had belonged to one sick or dead of the disease, if touched by some other living creature, not of the human species, were the occasion, not merely of sickening, but of an almost instantaneous death. Whereof my own eyes (as I said a little before) had cognisance, one day among others, by the following experience. The rags of a poor man who had died of the disease being strewn about the open street, two hogs came thither, and after, as is their wont, no little trifling with their snouts, took the rags between their teeth and tossed them to and fro about their chaps; whereupon, almost immediately, they gave a few turns, and fell down dead, as if by poison, upon the rags which in an evil hour they had disturbed.

In which circumstances, not to speak of many others of a similar or even graver complexion, divers apprehensions and imaginations were engendered in the minds of such as were left alive, inclining almost all of them to the same harsh resolution, to wit, to shun and abhor all contact with the sick and all that belonged to them, thinking thereby to make each his own health secure. Among whom there were those who thought that to live temperately and avoid all excess would count for much as a preservative against seizures of this kind. Wherefore they banded together, and, dissociating themselves from all others, formed communities in houses where there were no sick, and lived a separate and secluded life, which they regulated with the utmost care, avoiding every kind of luxury, but eating and drinking very moderately of the most delicate viands and the finest wines, holding converse with none but one another, lest tidings of sickness or death should reach them, and diverting their minds with music and such other delights as they could devise. Others, the bias of whose minds was in the opposite direction, maintained, that to drink freely, frequent places of public resort, and take their pleasure with song and revel, sparing to satisfy no appetite, and to laugh and mock at no event, was the sovereign remedy for so great an evil: and that which they affirmed they also put in practice, so far as they were able, resorting day and night, now to this tavern, now to that, drinking with an entire disregard of rule or measure, and by preference making the houses of others, as it were, their inns, if they but saw in them aught that was particularly to their taste or liking; which they were readily able to do, because the owners, seeing death imminent, had become as reckless of their property as of their lives; so that most of the houses were open to all comers, and no distinction was observed between the stranger who presented himself and the rightful lord. Thus, adhering ever to their inhuman determination to shun the sick, as far as possible, they ordered their life. In this extremity of our city's suffering and tribulation the venerable authority of laws, human and divine, was abased and all but totally dissolved, for lack of those who should have administered and enforced them, most of whom, like the rest of the citizens, were either dead or sick, or so hard bested for servants that they were unable to execute any office; whereby every man was free to do what was right in his own eyes.

Not a few there were who belonged to neither of the two said parties, but kept a middle course between them, neither laying the same restraint upon their diet as the former, nor allowing themselves the same license in drinking and other dissipations as the latter, but living with a degree of freedom sufficient to satisfy their appetites, and not as recluses. They therefore walked abroad, carrying in their hands flowers or fragrant herbs or divers sorts of spices, which they frequently raised to their noses, deeming it an excellent thing thus to comfort the brain with such perfumes, because the air seemed to be everywhere laden and reeking with the stench emitted by the dead and the dying and the odours of drugs.

Some again, the most sound, perhaps, in judgment, as they were also the most harsh in temper, of all, affirmed that there was no medicine for the disease superior or equal in efficacy to flight; following which prescription a multitude of men and women, negligent of all but themselves, deserted their city, their houses, their estate, their kinsfolk, their goods, and went into voluntary exile, or migrated to the country parts, as if God in visiting men with this pestilence in requital of their iniquities would not pursue them with His wrath, wherever they might be, but intended the destruction of such alone as remained within the circuit of the walls of the city; or deeming, perchance, that it was now time for all to flee from it, and that its last hour was come.

Of the adherents of these divers opinions not all died, neither did all escape; but rather there were, of each sort and in every place, many that sickened, and by those who retained their health were treated after the example which they themselves, while whole, had set, being everywhere left to languish in almost total neglect. Tedious were it to recount, how citizen avoided citizen, how among neighbours was scarce found any that shewed fellow-feeling for another, how kinsfolk held aloof, and never met, or but rarely; enough that this sore affliction entered so deep into the minds of men and women, that in the horror thereof brother was forsaken by brother, nephew by uncle, brother by sister, and oftentimes husband by wife; nay, what is more, and scarcely to be believed, fathers and mothers were found to abandon their own children, untended, unvisited, to their fate, as if they had been strangers. Wherefore the sick of both sexes, whose number could not be estimated, were left without resource but in the charity of friends (and few such there were), or the interest of servants, who were hardly to be had at high rates and on unseemly terms, and being, moreover, one and all men and women of gross understanding, and for the most part unused to such offices, concerned themselves no farther than to supply the immediate and expressed wants of the sick, and to watch them die; in which service they themselves not seldom perished with their gains. In consequence of which dearth of servants and dereliction of the sick by neighbours, kinsfolk and friends, it came to pass – a thing, perhaps, never before heard of that no woman, however dainty, fair or well-born she might be, shrank, when stricken with the disease, from the ministrations of a man, no matter whether he were young or no, or scrupled to expose to him every part of her body, with no more shame than if he had been a woman, submitting of necessity to that which her malady required; wherefrom, perchance, there resulted in after time some loss of modesty in such as recovered. Besides which many succumbed, who with proper attendance, would, perhaps, have escaped death; so that, what with the virulence of the plague and the lack of due tendance of the sick, the multitude of the deaths, that daily and nightly took place in the city, was such that those who heard the tale – not to say witnessed the fact – were struck dumb with amazement. Whereby, practices contrary to the former habits of the citizens could hardly fail to grow up among the survivors.

It had been, as to-day it still is, the custom for the women that were neighbours and of kin to the deceased to gather in his house with the women that were most closely connected with him, to wail with them in common, while on the other hand his male kinsfolk and neighbours, with not a few of the other citizens, and a due proportion of the clergy according to his quality, assembled without, in front of the house, to receive the corpse; and so the dead man was borne on the shoulders of his peers, with funeral pomp of taper and dirge, to the church selected by him before his death. Which rites, as the pestilence waxed in fury, were either in whole or in great part disused, and gave way to others of a novel order. For not only did no crowd of women surround the bed of the dying, but many passed from this life unregarded, and few indeed were they to whom were accorded the lamentations and bitter tears of sorrowing relations; nay, for the most part, their place was taken by the laugh, the jest, the festal gathering; observances which the women, domestic piety in large measure set aside, had adopted with very great advantage to their health. Few also there were whose bodies were attended to the church by more than ten or twelve of their neighbours, and those not the honourable and respected citizens; but a sort of corpse-carriers drawn from the baser ranks who called themselves becchini and performed such offices for hire, would shoulder the bier, and with hurried steps carry it, not to the church of the dead man's choice, but to that which was nearest at hand, with four or six priests in front and a candle or two, or, perhaps, none; nor did the priests distress themselves with too long and solemn an office, but with the aid of the becchini hastily consigned the corpse to the first tomb which they found untenanted. The condition of lower, and, perhaps, in great measure of the middle ranks, of the people shewed even worse and more deplorable; for, deluded by hope or constrained by poverty, they stayed in their quarters, in their houses, where they sickened by thousands a day, and, being without service or help of any kind, were, so to speak, irredeemably devoted to the death which overtook them. Many died daily or nightly in the public streets; of many others, who died at home, the departure was hardly observed by their neighbours, until the stench of their putrefying bodies carried the tidings; and what with their corpses and the corpses of others who died on every hand the whole place was a sepulchre.

It was the common practice of most of the neighbours, moved no less by fear of contamination by the putrefying bodies than by charity towards the deceased, to drag the corpses out of the houses with their own hands, aided, perhaps, by a porter, if a porter was to be had, and to lay them in front of the doors, where any one who made the round might have seen, especially in the morning, more of them than he could count; afterwards they would have biers brought up, or, in default, planks, whereon they laid them. Nor was it once or twice only that one and the same bier carried two or three corpses at once; but quite a considerable number of such cases occurred, one bier sufficing for husband and wife, two or three brothers, father and son, and so forth. And times without number it happened, that, as two priests, bearing the cross, were on their way to perform the last office for some one, three or four biers were brought up by the porters in rear of them, so that, whereas the priests supposed that they had but one corpse to bury, they discovered that there were six or eight, or sometimes more. Nor, for all their number, were their obsequies honoured by either tears or lights or crowds of mourners; rather, it was come to this, that a dead man was then of no more account than a dead goat would be to-day. From all which it is abundantly manifest, that that lesson of patient resignation, which the sages were never able to learn from the slight and infrequent mishaps which occur in the natural course of events, was now brought home even to the minds of the simple by the magnitude of their disasters, so that they became indifferent to them.

As consecrated ground there was not in extent sufficient to provide tombs for the vast multitude of corpses which day and night, and almost every hour, were brought in eager haste to the churches for interment, least of all, if ancient custom were to be observed and a separate resting-place assigned to each, they dug, for each graveyard, as soon as it was full, a huge trench, in which they laid the corpses as they arrived by hundreds at a time, piling them up as merchandise is stowed in the hold of a ship, tier upon tier, each covered with a little earth, until the trench would hold no more. But I spare to rehearse with minute particularity each of the woes that came upon our city, and say in brief, that, harsh as was the tenor of her fortunes, the surrounding country knew no mitigation, for there – not to speak of the castles, each, as it were, a little city in itself – in sequestered village, or on the open champaign, by the wayside, on the farm, in the homestead, the poor hapless husbandmen and their families, forlorn of physicians' care or servants' tendance, perished day and night alike, not as men, but rather as beasts. Wherefore, they too, like the citizens, abandoned all rule of life, all habit of industry, all counsel of prudence; nay, one and all, as if expecting each day to be their last, not merely ceased to aid Nature to yield her fruit in due season of their beasts and their lands and their past labours, but left no means unused, which ingenuity could devise, to waste their accumulated store; denying shelter to their oxen, asses, sheep, goats, pigs, fowls, nay, even to their dogs, man's most faithful companions, and driving them out into the fields to roam at large amid the unsheaved, nay, unreaped corn. Many of which, as if endowed with reason, took their fill during the day, and returned home at night without any guidance of herdsman. But enough of the country! What need we add, but (reverting to the city) that such and so grievous was the harshness of heaven, and perhaps in some degree of man, that, what with the fury of the pestilence, the panic of those whom it spared, and their consequent neglect or desertion of not a few of the stricken in their need, it is believed without any manner of doubt, that between March and the ensuing July upwards of a hundred thousand human beings lost their lives within the walls of the city of Florence, which before the deadly visitation would not have been supposed to contain so many people! How many grand palaces, how many stately homes, how many splendid residences, once full of retainers, of lords, of ladies, were now left desolate of all, even to the meanest servant! How many families of historic fame, of vast ancestral domains, and wealth proverbial, found now no scion to continue the succession! How many brave men, how many fair ladies, how many gallant youths, whom any physician, were he Galen, Hippocrates, or Aesculapius himself, would have pronounced in the soundest of health, broke fast with their kinsfolk, comrades and friends in the morning, and when evening came, supped with their forefathers in the other world.

The Plague in Elizabethan and Jacobean Times

There follows two plague poems from the Elizabethan and Jacobean eras, from John Davies and Thomas Nashe respectively.

John Davies (1569–1626) was born in Wiltshire and attended Winchester School, and thereafter secured a place to study at Queen's College, Oxford. It is unknown whether he actually received a degree but he went on to study at the Middle Temple and developed a reputation for being academically bright but badly behaved. While studying for a career in the law, he wrote poetry in his spare time and those poems brought him to the notice of Elizabeth I who appointed him to the position of Servant-in-Ordinary (a member of the royal household's legal staff). Soon he began eyeing a position in parliament and, in 1597, he was elected as the MP for Shaftesbury. He continued writing poetry but, like a good royal servant, afterwards dedicated several collections of his new poems to the queen. When James I ascended the throne, Davies ingratiated himself with the new king. He was, in fact, one of the representatives of the English court who travelled to Scotland to invite the new king to take the English throne on the death of Elizabeth. He enjoyed several government positions under the new Stuart regime and it is from during the reign of James I that this poem dates. The exact date of the poem remains unknown; it could have been inspired by the two outbreaks of plague in England in 1603 and 1626, both of which Davies would have lived to see. As is to be expected from pre-nineteenth-century sources, the poem exhibits a strong belief in the miasma theory; it is the foul vapours in London which have caused the plague.[16]

Thomas Nashe (1567–1601) was an Elizabethan poet, playwright and fiction writer. He is chiefly remembered as the author of a picaresque novel titled *The Unfortunate Traveller; or, The Life of Jack Wilton* (1594) and several other minor pieces. The Black Death in the fourteenth century by no means meant an end to plague outbreaks; successive outbreaks in England occurred over several successive centuries. There were outbreaks in London, for example, in 1563 and 1593. Although the date of the poem's composition cannot be given with certainty, it was perhaps the 1593 outbreak that inspired it; Nashe was living in London at the time and would have had first-hand knowledge of the disease. As readers can see, there is a clear moral message here: as the plague shows, one must serve God because this life is fleeting.[17]

'The Triumph of Death' by John Davies (c.1603)

London now smokes with vapors that arise
From his foule sweat, himselfe he so bestirres:
'Cast out your dead!' the carcase-carrier cries,
Which he by heapes in groundlesse graves interres. –

Now like to bees in summer's heate from hives,
Out flie the citizens, some here, some there;
Some all alone, and others with their wives:
With wives and children some flie, all for feare!

Here stands a watch, with guard of partizans,
To stoppe their passages, or to or fro,
As if they were not men, nor Christians,
But fiends or monsters, murdering as they go.

Each village, free, now stands upon her guard,
None must have harbour in them but their owne;
And as for life and death all watch and ward,
And flie for life (as death) the man unknowne!

Here crie the parents for their children's death,
There howle the children for the parents' losse,
And often die as they are drawing breath
To crie for their but now inflicted crosse.

The last survivor of a familie
Which yesterday, perhaps, were all in health,
Now dies to beare his fellowes companie,
And for a grave for all gives all their wealth.

The London lanes (thereby themselves to save)
Did vomit out their undigested dead,
Who by cart-loads are carried to the grave;
For all these lanes with folke were overfed.

The king himselfe (O wretched times the while!)
From place to place himselfe did flie,
Which from himselfe himselfe did seek t'exile,
Who (as amaz'd) not safe knew where to lie.

For hardly could one man another meete
That in his bosom brought not odious death;
It was confusion but a friend to greet,
For, like a fiend, he banned with his breath.

Now fall the people unto publike fast,
And all assemble in the church to pray;
Early and late their soules there take repast,
As if preparing for a later day.

The pastors now steep all their words in brine,
With ' woe, woe, woe,' – and nought is heard but woe
'Woe and alas!' (they say) 'the powers divine
'Are bent mankind, for shine, to overthrow!

'Repent, repent,' (like Jonas, now they crie)
'Ye men of England! O repent, repent,
To see if ye maie move pittie's eye
To look upon you ere you quite be spent.

And oft while he breathes out these bitter words,
He drawing breath draws in more bitter bane;
For now the aire no aire, but death affords,
And lights of art (for helpe) were in the wane.

The ceremonie at their burialls
Is' ashes but to ashes, dust to dust;
Nay, not so much; for strait the pitman falls
(If he can stand) to hide them as he must.

But if the pitman have not so much sense
To see nor feele which way the winde doth sit,
To take the same, he hardly comes from thence,
But for himself, perhaps, he makes the pit.

For look how leaves in autumn from the tree
With wind do fall, whose heaps fill holes in ground;
So might ye with the plague's breath people see
Fall by great heaps and fill up holes profound.

No holy turf was left to hide the head
Of holiest men; but most unhallow'd grounds,
Ditches, and highwaies, must receive the dead,
The dead (ah, woe the while!) so o'er abound.

Time never knew, since he begunne his houres,
(For aught we reade) a plague so long remaine
In any citie as this plague of ours;
For now six yeares in London it hath laine.

But thou in whose high hand all hearts are held,
Convert us, and from us this plague avert;
So sin shall yield to grace, and grace shall yield
The giver glory for so dear desert.

In few, what should I say? the best are nought
That breathe, since man first breathing did rebell:
The best that breathe are worse than may be thought
If thought can thinke, the best can do but well:
For none doth well on earth but such as will
Confesse, with griefe, they do exceeding ill.

'A Litany in Time of Plague' by Thomas Nashe (c.1592)

Adieu, farewell, earth's bliss;
This world uncertain is;
Fond are life's lustful joys;
Death proves them all but toys;
None from his darts can fly;
I am sick, I must die.
  Lord, have mercy on us!

Rich men, trust not in wealth,
Gold cannot buy you health;
Physic himself must fade.
All things to end are made,
The plague full swift goes by;
I am sick, I must die.
  Lord, have mercy on us!

Beauty is but a flower
Which wrinkles will devour;
Brightness falls from the air;

Queens have died young and fair;
Dust hath closed Helen's eye.
I am sick, I must die.
  Lord, have mercy on us!

Strength stoops unto the grave,
Worms feed on Hector brave;
Swords may not fight with fate,
Earth still holds open her gate.
'Come, come!' the bells do cry.
I am sick, I must die.
  Lord, have mercy on us!

Wit with his wantonness
Tasteth death's bitterness;
Hell's executioner
Hath no ears for to hear
What vain art can reply.
I am sick, I must die.
  Lord, have mercy on us!

Haste, therefore, each degree,
To welcome destiny;
Heaven is our heritage,
Earth but a player's stage;
Mount we unto the sky.
I am sick, I must die.
  Lord, have mercy on us!

Tales of the Plague and the Fire (1665–66)

The publication of Daniel Defoe's *Robinson Crusoe* in 1719 marked the birth of the English novel.[18] Although the genre had antecedents on the European continent – notably in seventeenth-century Spain with the publication of the somewhat ridiculous romance *Don Quixote* – the English novel aimed to represent 'real life.' Defoe went on to write several more novels including *A Journal of the Plague Year* in 1722. It is the fictional account of one man's experience of living in London during the Great Plague of London (1665–66), so called to distinguish it from the smaller outbreaks of plague in 1603, 1626 and 1636. So convincing was Defoe's realism in *A Journal of the Plague Year* – with his referencing of the Bills of Mortality, descriptions of London's environs, and his depiction of sick people's symptoms – that, upon its first publication in 1722, readers assumed it was a work of non-fiction. In fact, it was not until the novelist Walter Scott classified it properly as a historical novel in the nineteenth century that people began to accept its status as a work of fiction. Be that as it may, *A Journal of the Plague Year* makes for riveting reading. The extract presented here depicts a man's anxieties while seeing the numbers on the Bills of Mortality rise each week while struggling to decide whether he should stay in London or leave. Eventually the plague takes hold and London becomes eerily quiet.

From *A Journal of the Plague Year* by Daniel Defoe (1722)

Being Observations or Memorials
of the most remarkable occurrences,

as well public *as* private, which happened in
London during the last great visitation in 1665.
Written by a CITIZEN who continued
all the while in *London*.
Never made publick before (1722)

Daniel Defoe.

It was about the beginning of September, 1664, that I, among the rest of my neighbours, heard in ordinary discourse that the plague was returned again in Holland; for it had been very violent there, and particularly at Amsterdam and Rotterdam, in the year 1663, whither, they say, it was brought, some said from Italy, others from the Levant, among some goods which were brought home by their Turkey fleet; others said it was brought from Candia; others from Cyprus. It mattered not from whence it came; but all agreed it was come into Holland again.

We had no such thing as printed newspapers in those days to spread rumours and reports of things, and to improve them by the invention of men, as I have lived to see practised since. But such things as these were gathered from the letters of merchants and others who corresponded abroad, and from them was handed about by word of mouth only; so that things did not spread instantly over the whole nation, as they do now. But it seems that the Government had a true account of it, and several councils were held about ways to prevent its coming over; but all was kept very private. Hence it was that this rumour died off again, and people began to forget it as a thing we were very little concerned in, and that we hoped was not true; till the latter end of November or the beginning of December 1664 when two men, said to be Frenchmen, died of the plague in Long Acre, or rather at the upper end of Drury Lane. The family they were in endeavoured to conceal it as much as possible, but as it had gotten some vent in the discourse of the neighbourhood, the Secretaries of State got knowledge of it; and concerning themselves to inquire about it, in order to be certain of the truth, two physicians and a surgeon were ordered to go to the house and make inspection. This they did; and finding evident tokens of the sickness upon both the bodies that were dead, they gave their opinions publicly that they died of the plague. Whereupon it was given in to the parish clerk, and he also returned them to the Hall; and it was printed in the weekly bill of mortality in the usual manner, thus –

Plague, 2. Parishes infected, 1

The people showed a great concern at this, and began to be alarmed all over the town, and the more, because in the last week in December 1664 another man died in the same house, and of the same distemper. And then we were easy again for about six weeks, when none having died with any marks of infection, it was said the distemper was gone; but after that, I think it was about the 12th of February, another died in another house, but in the same parish and in the same manner.

This turned the people's eyes pretty much towards that end of the town, and the weekly bills showing an increase of burials in St Giles's parish more than usual, it began to be suspected that the plague was among the people at that end of the town, and that many had died of it, though they had taken care to keep it as much from the knowledge of the public as possible. This possessed the heads of the people very much, and few cared to go through Drury Lane, or the other streets suspected, unless they had extraordinary business that obliged them to it.

This increase of the bills stood thus: the usual number of burials in a week, in the parishes of St Giles-in-the-Fields and St Andrew's, Holborn, were from twelve to seventeen or nineteen each, few more or less; but from the time that the plague first began in St Giles's parish, it was observed that the ordinary burials increased in number considerably. For example: –

From December 27 to January 3	St Giles	16
	St Andrews	17
From January 3 to January 10	St Giles	12
	St Andrews	25
From January 10 to January 17	St Giles	18
	St Andrews	28
From January 17 to January 24	St Giles	23
	St Andrews	16
From January 24 to January 30	St Giles	24
	St Andrews	15
From January 30 to February 7	St Giles	24
	St Andrews	15
From February 7 to February 14	St Giles	24

The like increase of the bills was observed in the parishes of St Bride's, adjoining on one side of Holborn parish, and in the parish of St James, Clerkenwell, adjoining on the other side of Holborn; in both which parishes the usual numbers that died weekly were from four to six or eight, whereas at that time they were increased as follows: –

From December 20 to December 27	St Bride's	0
	St James	8
From December 27 to January 3	St Bride's	6
	St James	9
From January 3 to January 10	St Bride's	11
	St James	7
From January 10 to January 17	St Bride's	12
	St James	9
From January 17 to January 24	St Bride's	9
	St James	15
From January 24 to January 31	St Bride's	8
	St James	12

From January 31 to February 7	St Bride's St James	13 5
From February 7 to February 14	St Bride's St James	12 6

Besides this, it was observed with great uneasiness by the people that the weekly bills in general increased very much during these weeks, although it was at a time of the year when usually the bills are very moderate.

The usual number of burials within the bills of mortality for a week was from about 240 or thereabouts to 300. The last was esteemed a pretty high bill; but after this we found the bills successively increasing as follows: –

	Buried	**Increased**
From December the 20th to the 27th	291	…
From December the 27th to the 3rd January	349	58
From January the 3rd to the 10th of January	394	45
From January the 10th to the 17th of January	415	21
From January the 17th to the 24th of January	474	59

This last bill was really frightful, being a higher number than had been known to have been buried in one week since the preceding visitation of 1656.

However, all this went off again, and the weather proving cold, and the frost, which began in December, still continuing very severe even till near the end of February, attended with sharp though moderate winds, the bills decreased again, and the city grew healthy, and everybody began to look upon the danger as good as over; only that still the burials in St Giles's continued high. From the beginning of April especially they stood at twenty-five each week, till the week from the 18th to the 25th, when there was buried in St Giles's parish thirty, whereof two of the plague and eight of the spotted-fever, which was looked upon as the same thing; likewise the number that died of the spotted-fever in the whole increased, being eight the week before, and twelve the week above-named.

This alarmed us all again, and terrible apprehensions were among the people, especially the weather being now changed and growing warm, and the summer being at hand. However, the next week there seemed to be some hopes again; the bills were low, the number of the dead in all was but 388, there was none of the plague, and but four of the spotted-fever.

But the following week it returned again, and the distemper was spread into two or three other parishes, viz., St Andrew's, Holborn; St Clement Danes; and, to the great affliction of the city, one died within the walls, in the parish of St Mary Woolchurch, that is to say, in Bearbinder Lane, near Stocks Market; in all there were nine of the plague and six of the spotted-fever. It was, however, upon inquiry found that this Frenchman who died in Bearbinder Lane was one who, having lived in Long Acre, near the infected houses, had removed for fear of the distemper, not knowing that he was already infected.

This was the beginning of May, yet the weather was temperate, variable, and cool enough, and people had still some hopes. That which encouraged them was that the city was healthy: the whole ninety-seven parishes buried but fifty-four, and we began to hope that, as it was chiefly among the people at that end of the town, it might go no farther; and the rather, because the next week, which was from the 9th of May to the 16th, there died but three, of which not one within the whole city or liberties; and St Andrew's buried but fifteen, which was very low. 'Tis true St Giles's buried two-and-thirty, but still, as there was but one of the plague, people began to be easy. The whole bill also was very low, for the week before the bill was but 347, and the week above mentioned but 343. We continued in these hopes for a few days, but it was but for a few, for the people were no more to be deceived thus; they searched the houses and found that the plague was really spread every way, and that many died of it every day. So that now all our extenuations abated, and it was no more to be concealed; nay, it quickly appeared that the infection had spread itself beyond all hopes of abatement. That in the parish of St Giles it was gotten into several streets, and several families lay all sick together; and, accordingly, in the weekly bill for the next week the thing began to show itself. There was indeed but fourteen set down of the plague, but this was all knavery and collusion, for in St Giles's parish they buried forty in all, whereof it was certain most of them died of the plague, though they were set down of other distempers; and though the number of all the burials were not increased above thirty-two, and the whole bill being but 385, yet there was fourteen of the spotted-fever, as well as fourteen of the plague; and we took it for granted upon the whole that there were fifty died that week of the plague.

The next bill was from the 23rd of May to the 30th, when the number of the plague was seventeen. But the burials in St Giles's were fifty-three – a frightful number! – of whom they set down but nine of the plague; but on an examination more strictly by the justices of peace, and at the Lord Mayor's request, it was found there were twenty more who were really dead of the plague in that parish, but had been set down of the spotted-fever or other distempers, besides others concealed.

But those were trifling things to what followed immediately after; for now the weather set in hot, and from the first week in June the infection spread in a dreadful manner, and the bills rose high; the articles of the fever, spotted-fever, and teeth began to swell; for all that could conceal their distempers did it, to prevent their neighbours shunning and refusing to converse with them, and also to prevent authority shutting up their houses; which, though it was not yet practised, yet was threatened, and people were extremely terrified at the thoughts of it.

The second week in June, the parish of St Giles, where still the weight of the infection lay, buried 120, whereof though the bills said but sixty-eight of the plague, everybody said there had been 100 at least, calculating it from the usual number of funerals in that parish, as above.

Till this week the city continued free, there having never any died, except that one Frenchman whom I mentioned before, within the whole ninety-seven parishes. Now there died four within the city, one in Wood Street, one in Fenchurch Street, and two in Crooked Lane. Southwark was entirely free, having not one yet died on that side of the water.

I lived without Aldgate, about midway between Aldgate Church and Whitechappel Bars, on the left hand or north side of the street; and as the distemper had not reached to that side of the city, our neighbourhood continued very easy. But at the other end of the town their consternation was very great: and the richer sort of people, especially the nobility and gentry from the west part of the city, thronged out of town with their families and servants in an unusual manner; and this was more particularly seen in Whitechappel; that is to say, the Broad Street where I lived; indeed, nothing was to be seen but waggons and carts, with goods, women, servants, children, &c.; coaches filled with people of the better sort and horsemen attending them, and all hurrying away; then empty waggons and carts appeared, and spare horses with servants, who, it was apparent, were returning or sent from the countries to fetch more people; besides innumerable numbers of men on horseback, some alone, others with servants, and, generally speaking, all loaded with baggage and fitted out for travelling, as anyone might perceive by their appearance.

This was a very terrible and melancholy thing to see, and as it was a sight which I could not but look on from morning to night (for indeed there was nothing else of moment to be seen), it filled me with very serious thoughts of the misery that was coming upon the city, and the unhappy condition of those that would be left in it.

This hurry of the people was such for some weeks that there was no getting at the Lord Mayor's door without exceeding difficulty; there were such pressing and crowding there to get passes and certificates of health for such as travelled abroad, for without these there was no being admitted to pass through the towns upon the road, or to lodge in any inn. Now, as there had none died in the city for all this time, my Lord Mayor gave certificates of health without any difficulty to all those who lived in the ninety-seven parishes, and to those within the liberties too for a while.

This hurry, I say, continued some weeks, that is to say, all the month of May and June, and the more because it was rumoured that an order of the Government was to be issued out to place turnpikes and barriers on the road to prevent people travelling, and that the towns on the road would not suffer people from London to pass for fear of bringing the infection along with them, though neither of these rumours had any foundation but in the imagination, especially at-first.

I now began to consider seriously with myself concerning my own case, and how I should dispose of myself; that is to say, whether I should resolve to stay in London or shut up my house and flee, as many of my neighbours did. I have set this particular down so fully, because I know not but it may be of moment to those who come after me, if they come to be brought to the same distress, and to the same manner of making their choice; and therefore I desire this account may pass with them rather for a direction to themselves to act by than a history of my actings, seeing it may not be of one farthing value to them to note what became of me.

I had two important things before me: the one was the carrying on my business and shop, which was considerable, and in which was embarked all my effects in the world; and the other was the preservation of my life in so dismal a calamity as I saw apparently was coming upon the whole city, and which, however great it was, my fears perhaps, as well as other people's, represented to be much greater than it could be.

The first consideration was of great moment to me; my trade was a saddler, and as my dealings were chiefly not by a shop or chance trade, but among the merchants trading to the English colonies in America, so my effects lay very much in the hands of such. I was a single man, 'tis true, but I had a family of servants whom I kept at my business; had a house, shop, and warehouses filled with goods; and, in short, to leave them all as things in such a case must be left (that is to say, without any overseer or person fit to be trusted with them), had been to hazard the loss not only of my trade, but of my goods, and indeed of all I had in the world.

I had an elder brother at the same time in London, and not many years before come over from Portugal: and advising with him, his answer was in three words, the same that was given in another case quite different, viz., 'Master, save thyself.' In a word, he was for my retiring into the country, as he resolved to do himself with his family; telling me what he had, it seems, heard abroad, that the best preparation for the plague was to run away from it. As to my argument of losing my trade, my goods, or debts, he quite confuted me. He told me the same thing which I argued for my staying, viz., that I would trust God with my safety and health, was the strongest repulse to my pretensions of losing my trade and my goods; 'for', says he, 'is it not as reasonable that you should trust God with the chance or risk of losing your trade, as that you should stay in so eminent a point of danger, and trust Him with your life?'

I could not argue that I was in any strait as to a place where to go, having several friends and relations in Northamptonshire, whence our family first came from; and particularly, I had an only sister in Lincolnshire, very willing to receive and entertain me.

My brother, who had already sent his wife and two children into Bedfordshire, and resolved to follow them, pressed my going very earnestly; and I had once resolved to comply with his desires, but at that time could get no horse; for though it is true all the people did not go out of the city of London, yet I may venture to say that in a manner all the horses did; for there was hardly a horse to be bought or hired in the whole city for some weeks. Once I resolved to travel on foot with one servant, and, as many did, lie at no inn, but carry a soldier's tent with us, and so lie in the fields, the weather being very warm, and no danger from taking cold. I say, as many did, because several did so at last, especially those who had been in the armies in the war which had not been many years past; and I must needs say that, speaking of second causes, had most of the people that travelled done so, the plague had not been carried into so many country towns and houses as it was, to the great damage, and indeed to the ruin, of abundance of people.

But then my servant, whom I had intended to take down with me, deceived me; and being frighted at the increase of the distemper, and not knowing when I should go, he took other measures, and left me, so I was put off for that time; and, one way or other, I always found that to appoint to go away was always crossed by some accident or other, so as to disappoint and put it off again; and this brings in a story which otherwise might be thought a needless digression, viz., about these disappointments being from Heaven.

I mention this story also as the best method I can advise any person to take in such a case, especially if he be one that makes conscience of his duty, and would be directed what to do in it, namely, that he should keep his eye upon the particular providences which occur at that time, and look upon them complexly, as they regard one another, and as all together regard the question before him: and then, I think, he may safely take them for intimations from Heaven of what is his unquestioned duty to do in such a case; I mean as to going away from or staying in the place where we dwell, when visited with an infectious distemper.

It came very warmly into my mind one morning, as I was musing on this particular thing, that as nothing attended us without the direction or permission of Divine Power, so these disappointments must have something in them extraordinary; and I ought to consider whether it did not evidently point out, or intimate to me, that it was the will of Heaven I should not go. It immediately followed in my thoughts, that if it really was from God that I should stay, He was able effectually to preserve me in the midst of all the death and danger that would surround me; and that if I attempted to secure myself by fleeing from my habitation, and acted contrary to these intimations, which I believe to be Divine, it was a kind of flying from God, and that He could cause His justice to overtake me when and where He thought fit.

These thoughts quite turned my resolutions again, and when I came to discourse with my brother again I told him that I inclined to stay and take my lot in that station in which God had placed me, and that it seemed to be made more especially my duty, on the account of what I have said.

My brother, though a very religious man himself, laughed at all I had suggested about its being an intimation from Heaven, and told me several stories of such foolhardy people, as he called them, as I was; that I ought indeed to submit to it as a work of Heaven if I had been any way disabled by distempers or diseases, and that then not being able to go, I ought to acquiesce in the direction of Him, who, having been my Maker, had an undisputed right of sovereignty in disposing of me, and that then there had been no difficulty to determine which was the call of His providence and which was not; but that I should take it as an intimation from Heaven that I should not go out of town, only because I could not hire a horse to go, or my fellow was run away that was to attend me, was ridiculous, since at the time I had my health and limbs, and other servants, and might with ease travel a day or two on foot, and having a good certificate of being in perfect health, might either hire a horse or take post on the road, as I thought fit.

Then he proceeded to tell me of the mischievous consequences which attended the presumption of the Turks and Mahometans in Asia and in other places where he had been (for my brother, being a merchant, was a few years before, as I have already observed, returned from abroad, coming last from Lisbon), and how, presuming upon their professed predestinating notions, and of every man's end being predetermined and unalterably beforehand decreed, they would go unconcerned into infected places and converse with infected persons, by which means they died at the rate of ten or fifteen thousand a week, whereas the Europeans or Christian merchants, who kept themselves retired and reserved, generally escaped the contagion.

Upon these arguments my brother changed my resolutions again, and I began to resolve to go, and accordingly made all things ready; for, in short, the infection increased round me, and the bills were risen to almost seven hundred a week, and my brother told me he would venture to stay no longer. I desired him to let me consider of it but till the next day, and I would resolve: and as I had already prepared everything as well as I could as to MY business, and whom to entrust my affairs with, I had little to do but to resolve.

I went home that evening greatly oppressed in my mind, irresolute, and not knowing what to do. I had set the evening wholly – apart to consider seriously about it, and was all alone; for already people had, as it were by a general consent, taken up the custom of not going out of doors after sunset; the reasons I shall have occasion to say more of by-and-by.

In the retirement of this evening I endeavoured to resolve, first, what was my duty to do, and I stated the arguments with which my brother had pressed me to go into the country, and I set, against them the strong impressions which I had on my mind for staying; the visible call I seemed to have from the particular circumstance of my calling, and the care due from me for the preservation of my effects, which were, as I might say, my estate; also the intimations which I thought I had from Heaven, that to me signified a kind of direction to venture; and it occurred to me that if I had what I might call a direction to stay, I ought to suppose it contained a promise of being preserved if I obeyed.

This lay close to me, and my mind seemed more and more encouraged to stay than ever, and supported with a secret satisfaction that I should be kept. Add to this, that, turning over the Bible which lay before me, and while my thoughts were more than ordinarily serious upon the question, I cried out, 'Well, I know not what to do; Lord, direct me!' and the like; and at that juncture I happened to stop turning over the book at the ninety-first Psalm, and casting my eye on the second verse, I read on to the seventh verse exclusive, and after that included the tenth, as follows: 'I will say of the Lord, He is my refuge and my fortress: my God, in Him will I trust. Surely He shall deliver thee from the snare of the fowler, and from the noisome pestilence. He shall cover thee with His feathers, and under His wings shalt thou trust: His truth shall be thy shield and buckler. Thou shalt not be afraid for the terror by night; nor for the arrow that flieth by day; nor for the pestilence that walketh in darkness; nor for the destruction that wasteth at noonday. A thousand shall fall at thy side, and ten thousand at thy right hand; but it shall not come nigh thee. Only with thine eyes shalt thou behold and see the reward of the wicked. Because thou hast made the Lord, which is my refuge, even the most High, thy habitation; there shall no evil befall thee, neither shall any plague come nigh thy dwelling,' &C.

I scarce need tell the reader that from that moment I resolved that I would stay in the town, and casting myself entirely upon the goodness and protection of the Almighty, would not seek any other shelter whatever; and that, as my times were in His hands, He was as able to keep me in a time of the infection as in a time of health; and if He did not think fit to deliver me, still I was in His hands, and it was meet He should do with me as should seem good to Him.

With this resolution I went to bed; and I was further confirmed in it the next day by the woman being taken ill with whom I had intended to entrust my house and all my affairs. But I had a further obligation laid on me on the same side, for the next day I found myself very much out of order also, so that if I would have gone away, I could not, and I continued ill three or four days, and this entirely determined my stay; so I took my leave of my brother, who went away to Dorking, in

Surrey, and afterwards fetched a round farther into Buckinghamshire or Bedfordshire, to a retreat he had found out there for his family.

It was a very ill time to be sick in, for if any one complained, it was immediately said he had the plague; and though I had indeed no symptom of that distemper, yet being very ill, both in my head and in my stomach, I was not without apprehension that I really was infected; but in about three days I grew better; the third night I rested well, sweated a little, and was much refreshed. The apprehensions of its being the infection went also quite away with my illness, and I went about my business as usual.

These things, however, put off all my thoughts of going into the country; and my brother also being gone, I had no more debate either with him or with myself on that subject.

It was now mid-July, and the plague, which had chiefly raged at the other end of the town, and, as I said before, in the parishes of St Giles, St Andrew's, Holborn, and towards Westminster, began to now come eastward towards the part where I lived. It was to be observed, indeed, that it did not come straight on towards us; for the city, that is to say, within the walls, was indifferently healthy still; nor was it got then very much over the water into Southwark; for though there died that week 1268 of all distempers, whereof it might be supposed above 600 died of the plague, yet there was but twenty-eight in the whole city, within the walls, and but nineteen in Southwark, Lambeth parish included; whereas in the parishes of St Giles and St Martin-in-the-Fields alone there died 421.

But we perceived the infection kept chiefly in the out-parishes, which being very populous, and fuller also of poor, the distemper found more to prey upon than in the city, as I shall observe afterwards. We perceived, I say, the distemper to draw our way, viz., by the parishes of Clarkenwell, Cripplegate, Shoreditch, and Bishopsgate; which last two parishes joining to Aldgate, Whitechappel, and Stepney, the infection came at length to spread its utmost rage and violence in those parts, even when it abated at the western parishes where it began.

It was very strange to observe that in this particular week, from the 4th to the 11th of July, when, as I have observed, there died near 400 of the plague in the two parishes of St Martin and St Giles-in-the-Fields only, there died in the parish of Aldgate but four, in the parish of Whitechappel three, in the parish of Stepney but one.

Likewise in the next week, from the 11th of July to the 18th, when the week's bill was 1761, yet there died no more of the plague, on the whole Southwark side of the water, than sixteen. But this face of things soon changed, and it began to thicken in Cripplegate parish especially, and in Clarkenwell; so that by the second week in August, Cripplegate parish alone buried 886, and Clarkenwell 155. Of the first, 850 might well be reckoned to die of the plague; and of the last, the bill itself said 145 were of the plague.

During the month of July, and while, as I have observed, our part of the town seemed to be spared in comparison of the west part, I went ordinarily about the streets, as my business required, and particularly went generally once in a day, or in two days, into the city, to my brother's house, which he had given me charge of, and to see if it was safe; and having the key in my pocket, I used to go into the house, and over most of the rooms, to see that all was well; for though it be something wonderful to tell, that any should have hearts so hardened in the midst of such a calamity as to rob and steal, yet certain it is that all sorts of villainies, and even levities and debaucheries, were then practised in the town as openly as ever – I will not say quite as frequently, because the numbers of people were many ways lessened.

But the city itself began now to be visited too, I mean within the walls; but the number of people there were indeed extremely lessened by so great a multitude having been gone into the country; and even all this month of July they continued to flee, though not in such multitudes as formerly. In August, indeed, they fled in such a manner that I began to think there would be really none but magistrates and servants left in the city.

As they fled now out of the city, so I should observe that the Court removed early, viz., in the month of June, and went to Oxford, where it pleased God to preserve them; and the distemper did not, as I heard of, so much as touch them, for which I cannot say that I ever saw they showed any great token of thankfulness, and hardly anything of reformation, though they did not want being told that their crying vices might without breach of charity be said to have gone far in bringing that terrible judgement upon the whole nation.

The face of London was now indeed strangely altered: I mean the whole mass of buildings, city, liberties, suburbs, Westminster, Southwark, and altogether; for as to the particular part called the city, or within the walls, that was not yet much infected. But in the whole the face of things, I say, was much altered; sorrow and sadness sat upon every face; and though some parts were not yet overwhelmed, yet all looked deeply concerned; and, as we saw it apparently coming on, so every one looked on himself and his family as in the utmost danger. Were it possible to represent those times exactly to those that did not see them, and give the reader due ideas of the horror 'that everywhere presented itself, it must make just impressions upon their minds and fill them with surprise. London might well be said to be all in tears; the mourners did not go about the streets indeed, for nobody put on black or made a formal dress of mourning for their nearest friends; but the voice of mourners was truly heard in the streets. The shrieks of women and children at the windows and doors of their houses, where their dearest relations were perhaps dying, or just dead, were so frequent to be heard as we passed the streets, that it was enough to pierce the stoutest heart in the world to hear them. Tears and lamentations were seen almost in every house, especially in the first part of the visitation; for towards the latter end men's hearts were hardened, and death was so always before their eyes, that they did not so much concern themselves for the loss of their friends, expecting that themselves should be summoned the next hour.

Business led me out sometimes to the other end of the town, even when the sickness was chiefly there; and as the thing was new to me, as well as to everybody else, it was a most surprising thing to see those streets which were usually so thronged now grown desolate, and so few people to be seen in them, that if I had been a stranger and at a loss for my way, I might sometimes have gone the length of a whole street (I mean of the by-streets), and seen nobody to direct me except watchmen set at the doors of such houses as were shut up, of which I shall speak presently.

One day, being at that part of the town on some special business, curiosity led me to observe things more than usually, and indeed I walked a great way where I had no business. I went up Holborn, and there the street was full of people, but they walked in the middle of the great street, neither on one side or other, because, as I suppose, they would not mingle with anybody that came out of houses, or meet with smells and scent from houses that might be infected.

The Inns of Court were all shut up; nor were very many of the lawyers in the Temple, or Lincoln's Inn, or Gray's Inn, to be seen there. Everybody was at peace; there was no occasion for lawyers; besides, it being in the time of the vacation too, they were generally gone into the country. Whole rows of houses in some places were shut close up, the inhabitants all fled, and only a watchman or two left.

When I speak of rows of houses being shut up, I do not mean shut up by the magistrates, but that great numbers of persons followed the Court, by the necessity of their employments and other dependences; and as others retired, really frighted with the distemper, it was a mere desolating of some of the streets. But the fright was not yet near so great in the city, abstractly so called, and particularly because, though they were at first in a most inexpressible consternation, yet as I have observed that the distemper intermitted often at first, so they were, as it were, alarmed and unalarmed again, and this several times, till it began to be familiar to them; and that even when it appeared violent, yet seeing it did not presently spread into the city, or the east and south parts, the people began to take courage, and to be, as I may say, a little hardened. It is true a vast many people fled, as I have observed, yet they were chiefly from the west end of the town, and from that we call the heart of the city: that is to say, among the wealthiest of the people, and such people as were unencumbered with trades and business. But of the rest, the generality stayed, and seemed to abide the worst; so that in the place we call the Liberties, and in the suburbs, in Southwark, and in the east part, such as Wapping, Ratcliff, Stepney, Rotherhithe, and the like, the people generally stayed, except here and there a few wealthy families, who, as above, did not depend upon their business.

It must not be forgot here that the city and suburbs were prodigiously full of people at the time of this visitation, I mean at the time that it began; for though I have lived to see a further increase, and mighty throngs of people settling in London more than ever, yet we had always a notion that the numbers of people which, the wars being over, the armies disbanded, and the royal family and the monarchy being restored, had flocked to London to settle in business, or to depend upon and attend the Court for rewards of services, preferments, and the like, was such that the town was computed to have in it above a hundred thousand people more than ever it held before; nay, some took upon them to say it had twice as many, because all the ruined families of the royal party flocked hither. All the old soldiers set up trades here, and abundance of families settled here. Again, the Court brought with them a great flux of pride, and new fashions. All people were grown gay and luxurious, and the joy of the Restoration had brought a vast many families to London.

I often thought that as Jerusalem was besieged by the Romans when the Jews were assembled together to celebrate the Passover – by which means an incredible number of people were surprised there who would otherwise have been in other countries – so the plague entered London when an incredible increase of people had happened occasionally, by the particular circumstances above-named. As this conflux of the people to a youthful and gay Court made a great trade in the city, especially in everything that belonged to fashion and finery, so it drew by consequence a great number of workmen, manufacturers, and the like, being mostly poor people who depended upon their labour. And I remember in particular that in a representation to my Lord Mayor of the condition of the poor, it was estimated that there were no less than an hundred thousand riband-weavers in and about the city, the chiefest number of whom lived then in the parishes of Shoreditch, Stepney, Whitechappel, and Bishopsgate, that, namely, about Spitalfields; that is to say, as Spitalfields was then, for it was not so large as now by one fifth part.

By this, however, the number of people in the whole may be judged of; and, indeed, I often wondered that, after the prodigious numbers of people that went away at first, there was yet so great a multitude left as it appeared there was.

From *Old Saint Paul's* by William Harrison Ainsworth (1841)

William Harrison Ainsworth (1805–82) was an extremely popular author in the early Victorian period. Born in Manchester and originally destined for the legal profession, he was never the most devoted student and disappointed his family by pursuing writing. A number of successful hits marked the beginning of his literary career: *Rookwood* (1834), a novel which features as its hero the famous Dick Turpin; *Jack Sheppard* (1839), based upon the life of the eponymous eighteenth-century burglar; a Gothic romance titled *The Tower of London* (1840); and *Old Saint Paul's*, which was originally serialised in *The Times* and for which Ainsworth received a £1,000 advance.[19] *Old Saint Paul's*, an extract of which is included here, tells the story of the family of Stephen Bloundel who are living in London when the plague breaks out. Seeking to avoid the plague, the family go into self-imposed quarantine. Ainsworth's descriptions of an eerily quiet London and his morbid scenes of death and sickness are almost apocalyptic in nature. His model is clearly Defoe, whose account of the plague in *Journal of the Plague Year* (1722) he had read in depth and taken many details from. The extract below describes the plague at the beginning of the novel and, later on, the disease at its height.[20]

The Progress of the Pestilence

Towards the middle of May, the bills of mortality began to swell greatly in amount, and though but few were put down to the plague, and a large number to the spotted fever (another frightful disorder raging at the period), it is well known that the bulk had died of the former disease. The rigorous measures adopted by the authorities (whether salutary or not has been questioned), in shutting up houses and confining the sick and sound within them for forty days, were found so intolerable, that most persons were disposed to run any risk rather than be subjected to such a grievance, and every artifice was resorted to for concealing a case when it occurred. Hence, it seldom happened, unless by accident, that a discovery was made. Quack doctors were secretly consulted, instead of the regular practitioners; the searchers were bribed to silence; and large fees were given to the undertakers and buriers to lay the deaths to the account of some other disorder. All this, however, did not blind the eyes of the officers to the real state of things. Redoubling their vigilance, they entered houses on mere suspicion; inflicted punishments where they found their orders disobeyed or neglected; sent the sound to prison, – the sick to the pest-house; and replaced the faithless searchers by others upon whom they could place reliance. Many cases were thus detected; but in spite of every precaution, the majority escaped; and the vent was no sooner stopped in one quarter than it broke out with additional violence in another.

By this time the alarm had become general. All whose business or pursuits permitted it, prepared to leave London, which they regarded as a devoted city, without delay. As many houses were, therefore, closed from the absence of the inhabitants as from the presence of the plague, and this added to the forlorn appearance of the streets, which in some quarters were almost deserted. For a while, nothing was seen at the great outlets of the city but carts, carriages, and other vehicles, filled with goods and movables, on their way to the country; and, as may be supposed, the departure of their friends did not tend to abate the dejection of those whose affairs compelled them to remain behind.

One circumstance must not be passed unnoticed, namely, the continued fineness and beauty of the weather. No rain had fallen for upwards of three weeks. The sky was bright and cloudless; the atmosphere, apparently, pure and innoxious; while the heat was as great as is generally experienced in the middle of summer. But instead of producing its usual enlivening effect on the spirits, the fine weather added to the general gloom and apprehension, inasmuch as it led to the belief (afterwards fully confirmed), that if the present warmth was so pernicious, the more sultry seasons which were near at hand would aggravate the fury of the pestilence. Sometimes, indeed, when the deaths were less numerous, a hope began to be entertained that the distemper was abating, and confidence was for a moment restored; but these anticipations were speedily checked by the reappearance of the scourge, which seemed to baffle and deride all human skill and foresight.

London now presented a lamentable spectacle. Not a street but had a house in it marked with a red cross – some streets had many such. The bells were continually tolling for burials, and the dead-carts went their melancholy rounds at night and were constantly loaded. Fresh directions were issued by the authorities; and as domestic animals were considered to be a medium of conveying the infection, an order, which was immediately carried into effect, was given to destroy all dogs and cats. But this plan proved prejudicial rather than the reverse, as the bodies of the poor animals, most of which were drowned in the Thames, being washed ashore, produced a horrible and noxious effluvium, supposed to contribute materially to the propagation of the distemper.

No precautionary measure was neglected; but it may be doubted whether any human interference could have averted the severity of the scourge, which, though its progress might be checked for a few days by attention, or increased in the same ratio by neglect, would in the end have unquestionably fulfilled its mission. The College of Physicians, by the king's command, issued simple and intelligible directions, in the mother tongue, for the sick. Certain of their number, amongst whom was the reader's acquaintance, Doctor Hodges, were appointed to attend the infected; and two out of the Court of Aldermen were required to see that they duly executed their dangerous office. Public prayers and a general fast were likewise enjoined. But Heaven seemed deaf to the supplications of the doomed inhabitants – their prayers being followed by a fearful increase of deaths. A vast crowd was collected within Saint Paul's to hear a sermon preached by Doctor Sheldon, Archbishop of Canterbury, – a prelate greatly distinguished during the whole course of the visitation, by his unremitting charity and attention to the sick; and before the discourse was concluded, several fell down within the sacred walls, and, on being conveyed to their own homes, were found to be infected. On the following day, too, many others who had been present were seized with the disorder.

A fresh impulse was given to the pestilence from an unlooked for cause. It has been mentioned that the shutting up of houses and seclusion of the sick were regarded as an intolerable grievance, and though most were compelled to submit to it, some few resisted, and tumults and disturbances ensued. As the plague increased, these disturbances became more frequent, and the mob always taking part against the officers, they were frequently interrupted in the execution of their duty.

About this time a more serious affray than usual occurred, attended-with loss of life and other unfortunate consequences, which it may be worth while to relate, as illustrative of the peculiar state of the times. The wife of a merchant, named Barcroft, residing in Lothbury, being attacked by the plague, the husband, fearing his house would be shut up, withheld all information from the examiners and searchers. His wife died, and immediately afterwards one of his children was attacked. Still he refused to give notice. The matter, however, got wind. The searchers arrived at night, and being refused admittance, they broke into the house. Finding undoubted evidence of infection, they ordered it to be closed, stationed a watchman at the door, and marked it with the fatal sign. Barcroft remonstrated against their proceedings, but in vain. They told him he might think himself well off that he was not carried before the Lord Mayor, who would undoubtedly send him to Ludgate; and with other threats to the like effect, they departed.

The unfortunate man's wife and child were removed the following night in the dead-cart, and, driven half-mad by grief and terror, he broke open the door of his dwelling, and, plunging a sword in the watchman's breast, who opposed his flight, gained the street. A party of the watch happened to be passing at the time, and the fugitive was instantly secured. He made a great clamour, however, – calling to his neighbours and the bystanders to rescue him, and in another moment the watch was beaten off, and Barcroft placed on a post, whence he harangued his preservers on the severe restraints imposed upon the citizens, urging them to assist in throwing open the doors of all infected houses, and allowing free egress to their inmates.

Greedily listening to this insane counsel, the mob resolved to act upon it. Headed by the merchant, they ran down Thread-needle-street, and, crossing Stock's Market, burst open several houses in Bearbinder-lane, and drove away the watchmen. One man, more courageous than the others, tried to maintain his post, and was so severely handled by his assailants, that he died a few days afterwards of the injuries he had received. Most of those who had been imprisoned within their dwellings immediately issued forth, and joining the mob, which received fresh recruits each moment, started on the same errand.

Loud shouts were now raised of – 'Open the doors! No plague prisoners! No plague prisoners!' and the mob set off along the Poultry. They halted, however, before the Great Conduit, near the end of Bucklersbury, and opposite Mercer's Hall, because they perceived a company of the Train-bands advancing to meet them. A council of war was held, and many of the rabble were disposed to fly; but Barcroft again urged them to proceed, and they were unexpectedly added by Solomon Eagle, who, bursting through their ranks, with his brazier on his head, crying, 'Awake! sleepers, awake! the plague is at your doors! awake!' speeded towards the Train-bands, scattering sparks of fire as he pursued his swift career. The mob instantly followed, and, adding their shouts to his outcries, dashed on with such fury that the Train-bands did not dare to oppose them, and, after a slight and ineffectual resistance, were put to rout.

Barcroft, who acted as leader, informed them that there was a house in Wood-street shut up, and the crowd accompanied him thither. In a few minutes they had reached Bloundel's shop, but finding no one on guard – for the watchman, guessing their errand, had taken to his heels – they smeared over the fatal cross and inscription with a pail of mud gathered from the neighbouring kennel, and then broke open the door. The grocer and his apprentice hearing the disturbance, and being greatly alarmed at it, hurried to the shop, and found it full of people.

'You are at liberty Mr. Bloundel,' cried the merchant, who was acquainted with the grocer. 'We are determined no longer to let our families be imprisoned at the pleasure of the Lord Mayor and aldermen. We mean to break open all the plague houses, and set free their inmates.'

'For Heaven's sake, consider what you are about, Mr. Barcroft,' cried the grocer. 'My house has been closed for nearly a month. Nay, as my son has entirely recovered, and received his certificate of health from Doctor Hodges, it would have been opened in three days hence by the officers; so that I have suffered all the inconvenience of the confinement, and can speak to it. It is no doubt very irksome, and may be almost intolerable to persons of an impatient temperament: but I firmly believe it is the only means to check the progress of contagion. Listen to me, Mr. Barcroft – listen to me, good friends, and hesitate before you violate laws which have been made expressly to meet this terrible emergency.'

Here he was checked by loud groans and upbraidings from the bystanders.

'He tells you himself that the period of his confinement is just over,' cried Barcroft. 'It is plain he has no interest in the matter, except that he would have others suffer as he has done. Heed him not, my friends; but proceed with the good work. Liberate the poor plague prisoners. Liberate them. On! on!'

'Forbear, rash men,' cried Bloundel, in an authoritative voice. 'In the name of those you are bound to obey, I command you to desist.'

'Command us!' cried one of the bystanders, raising his staff in a menacing manner. 'Is this your gratitude for the favour we have just conferred upon you? Command us, forsooth! You had better repeat the order, and see how it will be obeyed.'

'I *do* repeat it,' rejoined the grocer, firmly. 'In the Lord Mayor's name, I command you to desist, and return to your homes.'

The man would have struck him with his staff, if he had not been himself felled to the ground by Leonard. This was the signal for greater outrage. The grocer and his apprentice were instantly assailed by several others of the mob, who, leaving them both on the floor covered with bruises, helped themselves to all they could lay hands on in the shop, and then quitted the premises.

It is scarcely necessary to track their course further; and it may be sufficient to state, that they broke open upwards of fifty houses in different streets. Many of the plague-stricken joined them, and several half-naked creatures were found dead in the streets on the following morning. Two houses in Blackfriars-lane were set on fire, and the conflagration was with difficulty checked; nor was it until late on the following day that the mob could be entirely dispersed. The originator of the disturbance, Barcroft, after a desperate resistance, was shot through the head by a constable.

The result of this riot, as will be easily foreseen, was greatly to increase the pestilence; and many of those who had been most active in it perished in prison of the distemper. Far from being discouraged by the opposition offered to their decrees, the city authorities enforced them with greater rigour than ever, and, doubling the number of the watch, again shut up all those houses which had been broken open during the late tumult.

Bloundel received a visit from the Lord Mayor, Sir John Lawrence, who, having been informed of his conduct, came to express his high approval of it, offering to remit the few days yet unexpired of his quarantine. The grocer, however, declined the offer, and with renewed expressions of approbation, Sir John Lawrence took his leave.

Three days afterwards, the Examiner of Health pronounced the grocer's house free from infection. The fatal mark was obliterated from the door; the shutters were unfastened; and Bloundel resumed his business as usual. Words are inadequate to describe the delight that filled the breast of every member of his family, on their first meeting after their long separation. It took place in the room adjoining the shop. Mrs. Bloundel received the joyful summons from Leonard, and, on descending with her children, found her husband and her son Stephen anxiously expecting her. Scarcely able to make up her mind as to which of the two she should embrace first, Mrs. Bloundel was decided by the pale countenance of her son, and rushing towards him, she strained him to her breast, while Amabel flew to her father's arms. The grocer could not repress his tears; but they were tears of joy, and that night's happiness made him ample amends for all the anxiety he had recently undergone.

'Well, Stephen, my dear child,' said his mother, as soon as the first tumult of emotion had subsided, – 'well, Stephen,' she said, smiling at him through her tears, and almost smothering him with kisses, 'you are not so much altered as I expected; and I do not think, if I had had the care of you, I could have nursed you better myself. You owe your father a second life, and we all owe him the deepest gratitude for the care he has taken of you.'

'I can never be sufficiently grateful for his kindness,' returned Stephen, affectionately.

'Give thanks to the beneficent Being who has preserved you from this great danger, my son, not to me,' returned Bloundel. 'The first moments of our reunion should be worthily employed.'

So saying, he summoned the household, and, for the first time for a month, the whole family party assembled, as before, at prayer. Never were thanksgivings more earnestly, more devoutly uttered. All arose with bright and cheerful countenances; and even Blaize seemed to have shaken off his habitual dread of the pestilence. As he retired with Patience, he observed to her, 'Master Stephen looks quite well, though a little thinner. I must ascertain from him the exact course of treatment pursued by his father. I wonder whether Mr. Bloundel would nurse *me* if I were to be suddenly seized with the distemper?'

'If he wouldn't, I *would*,' replied Patience.

'Thank you, thank you,' replied Blaize. 'I begin to think we shall get through it. I shall go out to-morrow and examine the bills of mortality, and see what progress the plague is making. I am all anxiety to know. I must get a fresh supply of medicine, too. My private store is quite gone, except three of my favourite refuses, which I shall take before I go to bed to-night. Unluckily, my purse is as empty as my phials.'

'I can lend you a little money,' said Patience. 'I haven't touched my last year's wages. They are quite at your service.'

'You are too good,' replied Blaize; 'but I won't decline the offer. I heard a man crying a new anti-pestilential elixir, as he passed the house yesterday. I must find him out and buy a bottle. Besides, I must call on my friend Parkhurst, the apothecary. – You are a good girl, Patience, and I'll marry you as soon as the plague ceases.'

'I have something else to give you,' rejoined Patience. 'This little bag contains a hazel-nut, from which I have picked the kernel, and filled its place with quicksilver, stopping the hole with wax. Wear it round your neck, and you will find it a certain preservative against the pestilence.'

'Who told you of this remedy?' asked Blaize, taking the bag.

'Your mother,' returned Patience.

'I wonder I never heard of it,' said the porter.

'She wouldn't mention it to you, because the doctor advised her not to put such matters into your head,' replied Patience. 'But I couldn't help indulging you. Heigho! I hope the plague will soon be over.'

'It won't be over for six months,' rejoined Blaize, shaking his head. 'I read in a little book, published in 1593, in Queen Elizabeth's reign, and written by Simon Kelway, 'that when little children flock together, and pretend that some of their number are dead, solemnizing the burial in a mournful sort, it is a certain token that a great mortality is at hand.' This I have myself seen more than once. Again, just before the great sickness of 1625, the churchyard wall of St. Andrew's, Holborn, fell down. I need not tell you that the same thing occurred after the frost this winter.'

'I heard of it,' replied Patience: 'but I did not know it was a bad sign.'

'It is a dreadful sign,' returned Blaize, with a shudder 'The thought of it brings back my old symptoms. I must have a supper to guard against infection – a slice of toasted bread, sprinkled with vinegar, and powdered with nutmeg.'

And chattering thus, they proceeded to the kitchen.

Before supper could be served, Dr. Hodges made his appearance. He was delighted to see the family assembled together again, and expressed a hearty wish that they might never more be divided. He watched Amabel and Leonard carefully, and seemed annoyed that the former rather shunned than favoured the regards of the apprentice.

Leonard, too, looked disconcerted; and though he was in possession of his mistress's promise, he did not like to reclaim it.

During the whole of the month, he had been constantly on the watch, and had scarcely slept at night, so anxious was he to prevent the possibility of any communication taking place between Rochester and his mistress. But, in spite of all his caution, it was possible he might be deceived. And when on this, their first meeting, she returned his anxious gaze with averted looks, he felt all his jealous misgivings return.

Supper, meanwhile, proceeded. Doctor Hodges was in excellent spirits, and drank a bottle of old sack with great relish. Overcome by the sight of his wife and children, the grocer abandoned himself to his feelings. As to his wife, she could scarcely contain herself, but wept and laughed by turns – now embracing her husband, now her son, between whom she had placed herself. Nor did she forget Doctor Hodges; and such was the exuberance of her satisfaction, that when the repast was ended, she arose, and, flinging her arms about his neck, termed him the preserver of her son.

'If any one is entitled to that appellation it is his father,' replied Hodges, 'and I may say, that in all my experience I have never witnessed such generous self-devotion as Mr. Bloundel has exhibited towards his son. You must now be satisfied, madam, that no person can so well judge what is proper for the safety of his family as your husband.'

'I never doubted it, sir,' replied Mrs. Bloundel.

'I must apprise you, then, that he has conceived a plan by which he trusts to secure you and his children and household from any future attack,' returned Hodges.

'I care not what it is, so it does not separate me from him,' replied Mrs. Bloundel.

'It does not,' replied the grocer. 'It will knit us more closely together than we have yet been. I mean to shut up my house, having previously stored it with provisions for a twelvemonth, and shall suffer no member of my family to stir forth as long as the plague endures.'

'I am ready to remain within doors, if it continues twenty years,' replied his wife. 'But how long do you think it *will* last, doctor?'

'Till next December, I have no doubt,' returned Hodges.

The Plague at its Height

[Months passed and] everything proceeded as before within his quiet dwelling; and, except that the family were diminished in number, all appeared the same. It is true they wanted the interest, and indeed the occupation, afforded them by the gentle invalid, but in other respects, no difference was observable. Devotional exercises, meals, the various duties of the house, and cheerful discourse, filled up the day, which never proved wearisome. The result proved the correctness of Mr. Bloundel's judgment. While the scourge continued weekly to extend its ravages throughout the city, it never crossed his threshold; and, except suffering in a slight degree from scorbutic affections, occasioned by the salt meats to which they were now confined, and for which the lemon and lime-juice, provided against such a contingency, proved an efficacious remedy, all the family enjoyed perfect health…

And now every other consideration was merged in the alarm occasioned by the daily increasing fury of the pestilence. Throughout July the excessive heat of the weather underwent no abatement, but in place of the clear atmosphere that had prevailed during the preceding month, unwholesome blights filled the air, and, confining the pestilential effluvia, spread the contagion far and wide with extraordinary rapidity. Not only was the city suffocated with heat, but filled with noisome smells, arising from the carcasses with which the close alleys and other out-of-the-way places were crowded, and which were so far decomposed as not to be capable of removal. The aspect of the river was as much changed as that of the city. Numbers of bodies were thrown into it, and, floating up with the tide, were left to taint the air on its banks, while strange, ill-omened fowl, attracted thither by their instinct, preyed upon them. Below the bridge, all captains of ships moored in the Pool, or off Wapping, held as little communication as possible with those on shore, and only received fresh provisions with the greatest precaution. As the plague increased, most of these removed lower down the river, and many of them put out entirely to sea. Above the bridge, most of the wherries and other smaller craft had disappeared, their owners having taken them up the river, and moored them against its banks at different spots, where they lived in them under tilts. Many hundreds of persons remained upon the river in this way during the whole continuance of the visitation.

August had now arrived, but the distemper knew no cessation. On the contrary, it manifestly increased in violence and malignity. The deaths rose a thousand in each week, and in the last week in this fatal month amounted to upwards of sixty thousand!

But, terrible as this was, the pestilence had not yet reached its height. Hopes were entertained that when the weather became cooler, its fury would abate; but these anticipations were fearfully disappointed. The bills of mortality rose the first week in September to seven thousand, and though they slightly decreased during the second week – awakening a momentary hope – on the third they advanced to twelve thousand! In less than ten days, upwards of two thousand persons perished in the parish of Aldgate alone; while Whitechapel suffered equally severely. Out of the hundred parishes in and about the city, one only, that of Saint John the Evangelist in Watling-street, remained uninfected, and this merely because there was scarcely a soul left within it, the greater part of the inhabitants having quitted their houses, and fled into the country.

The deepest despair now seized upon all the survivors. Scarcely a family but had lost half of its number – many, more than half – while those who were left felt assured that their turn would speedily arrive. Even the reckless were appalled, and abandoned their evil courses. Not only were the dead lying in the passages and alleys, but even in the main thoroughfares, and none would remove them. The awful prediction of Solomon Eagle that 'grass would grow in the streets, and that the living should not be able to bury the dead,' had come to pass. London had become one vast lazar-house, and seemed in a fair way of becoming a mighty sepulchre.

During all this time, Saint Paul's continued to be used as a pest-house, but it was not so crowded as heretofore, because, as not one in fifty of the infected recovered when placed under medical care, it was not thought worth while to remove them from their own abodes. The number of attendants, too, had diminished. Some had died, but the greater part had abandoned their offices from a fear of sharing the fate of their patients. In consequence of these changes, Judith Malmayns had been advanced to the post of chief nurse at the cathedral. Both she and Chowles had been attacked by the plague, and both had recovered. Judith attended the coffin-maker, and it was mainly owing to her that he got through the attack. She never left him for a moment, and would never suffer any one to approach him – a necessary precaution, as he was so much alarmed by his situation that he would infallibly have made some awkward revelations. When Judith, in her turn, was seized, Chowles exhibited no such consideration for her, and scarcely affected to conceal his disappointment at her recovery. This want of feeling on his part greatly incensed her against him, and though he contrived in some degree to appease her, it was long before she entirely forgave him. Far from being amended by her sufferings, she seemed to have grown more obdurate, and instantly commenced a fresh career of crime. It was not, however, necessary now to hasten the end of the sick. The distemper had acquired such force and malignity that it did its work quickly enough – often too quickly – and all she sought was to obtain possession of the poor patients' attire, or any valuables they might possess worth appropriating. To turn to the brighter side of the picture, it must not be omitted that when the pestilence was at its height, and no offers could induce the timorous to venture forth, or render assistance to the sufferers, Sir John Lawrence the Lord Mayor, the Duke of Albermarle, the Earl of Craven, and the Archbishop of Canterbury, devoted themselves to the care of the infected, and supplied them with every necessary they required. Among the physicians, no one deserves more honourable mention than Doctor Hodges, who was unremitting in his attentions to the sufferers.

To return to the grocer. While the plague was thus raging around him, and while every house in Wood-street except one or two, from which the inmates had fled, was attacked by the pestilence, he and his family had remained untouched. About the middle of August, he experienced a great alarm. His second son, Hubert, fell sick, and he removed him to one of the upper rooms which he had set aside as an hospital, and attended upon him himself. In a few days, however, his fears were removed and he found, to his great satisfaction, that the youth had not been attacked by the plague, but was only suffering from a slight fever, which quickly yielded to the remedies applied. About the same time, too, he lost his porter, Dallison. The poor fellow did not make his appearance as usual for two days, and intelligence of his fate was brought on the following day by his wife, who came to state that her husband was dead, and had been thrown into the plague-pit at Aldgate. The same night, however, she brought another man, named Allestry, who took the place of the late porter, and acquainted his employer with the deplorable state of the city.

Two days afterwards, Allestry himself died, and Mr. Bloundel had no one to replace him. He thus lost all means of ascertaining what was going forward; but the deathlike stillness around him, broken only by the hoarse tolling of a bell, by a wild shriek or other appalling cry, proclaimed too surely the terrible state of things. Sometimes, too, a passenger would go by, and would tell him the dreadful height to which the bills of mortality had risen, assuring him that ere another month had expired, not a soul would be left alive in London…

On the tenth of September, which was afterwards accounted the most fatal day of this fatal month, a young man of a very dejected appearance, and wearing the traces of severe suffering in his countenance, entered the west end of London, and took his way slowly towards the city. He had passed Saint Giles's without seeing a single living creature, or the sign of one in any of the houses. The broad thoroughfare was completely grown over with grass, and the habitations had the most melancholy and deserted air imaginable. Some doors and windows were wide open, discovering rooms with goods and furniture scattered about, having been left in this state by their inmates; but most part of them were closely fastened up.

As he proceeded along Holborn, the ravages of the scourge were yet more apparent. Every house, on either side of the way, had a red cross, with the fatal inscription above it, upon the door. Here and there, a watchman might be seen, looking more like a phantom than a living thing. Formerly, the dead were conveyed away at night, but now the carts went about in the daytime. On reaching Saint Andrew's, Holborn, several persons were seen wheeling hand-barrows filled with corpses, scarcely covered with clothing, and revealing the blue and white stripes of the pestilence, towards a cart which was standing near the church gates. The driver of the vehicle, a tall, cadaverous-looking man, was ringing his bell, and jesting with another person, whom the young man recognised, with a shudder, as Chowles. The coffin-maker also recognised him at the same moment, and called to him, but the other paid no attention to the summons and passed on.

Crossing Holborn Bridge, he toiled faintly up the opposite hill, for he was evidently suffering from extreme debility, and on gaining the summit was obliged to support himself against a wall for a few minutes, before he could proceed. The same frightful evidences of the ravages of the pestilence were observable here, as elsewhere. The houses were all marked with the fatal cross, and shut up. Another dead-cart was heard rumbling along, accompanied by the harsh cries of the driver, and the doleful ringing of the bell. The next moment the loathly vehicle was seen coming along the Old Bailey. It paused before a house, from which four bodies were brought, and then passed on towards Smithfield. Watching its progress with fearful curiosity, the young man noted how often it paused to increase its load. His thoughts, coloured by the scene, were of the saddest and dreariest complexion. All around wore the aspect of death. The few figures in sight seemed staggering towards the grave, and the houses appeared to be plague-stricken like the inhabitants. The heat was intolerably oppressive, and the air tainted with noisome exhalations. Ever and anon, a window would be opened, and a ghastly face thrust from it, while a piercing shriek, or lamentable cry, was uttered. No business seemed going on – there were no passengers – no vehicles in the streets. The mighty city was completely laid prostrate.

From 'A Tale of the Great Plague' by Thomas Hood (c.1840)

Thomas Hood (1799–1845) was born in London and, his father being a bookseller, he grew up around books. He went on to become a poet, novelist and satirist. Most famous for his poetry, Thomas Hood was declared by William Michael Rossetti in 1903 as 'the finest English poet' between the generations of Shelley and Tennyson.' While several of the works reproduced in this volume are serious in their tone, this particular short story takes a somewhat lighter approach to portraying a pandemic.[21]

'This is one of the *pest* discretions.' – SIR HUGH EVANS.

About five or six years after that deplorable great Plague of London, there befell a circumstance which, as it is not set forth in Defoe his history of the pestilence, I shall make bold to write down herein, not only on account of the strangeness of the event, but also because it carries a moral pick-a-back, as a good story ought to do.

It is a notoriously known fact, as collected from the bills of mortality, that there died of the plague in the mere metropolis a matter of some hundreds of thousands of human souls; yet notwithstanding this most awful warning to evil doers, the land did nevertheless bring forth such a rank crop of sin and wickedness, that the like was never known before or after; the City of London, especially, being overrun with bands of thieves and murtherers, against whom there was little or no check, the civical police having been utterly disbanded and disrupt during the ravages of the pestilence. Neither did men's minds turn for some time towards the mere safeguard of property, being still distracted with personal fears, for although the pest had, as it were, died of the excess of its own violence, yet from time to time there arose flying rumours of fresh breakings out of the malady. The small-pox and the malignant fever being the prolific parents of such like alarms. Accordingly many notable robberies and divers grievous murthers having been acted with impunity during the horrible crisis of the pest, those which had before been wicked were now hardened, and became a thousand times worse, till the city and the neighbourhood thereof seemed given in prey to devils, who had been loosened for a season from the everlasting fetters of the law.

Now four of these desperadoes having met together at the Dolphin in Deptford, they laid a plot together to rob a certain lone mansion house which stood betwixt the Thames marshes and the Forest of Hainault, and which was left in the charge of only one man, the family being gone off to another mansion house in the county of Wiltshire, for the sake of a more wholesome air. And the manner of the plot was this: one of the villains going in a feigned voice was to knock at the front-door and beg piteously for a night's shelter, and then the door, being opened, the other knaves were to rush in and bind the serving-man, or murther him, as might seem best, and so taking his keys they were to ransack the house, where they expected to find a good store of plate. Accordingly, one Friday, at the dead of the night, they set forth, having for leader a fellow that was named Blackface, by reason of a vizard which he wore always on such errands, diverting themselves by the way with laying out each man his share of the booty in the manner that pleased him best, wine and the women of Lewkener's Lane coming in you may be sure for the main burthen of the song. At last they entered the fore-court of the house which they were to rob, and which was as silent as death, and as dark, excepting a glimmer from one window towards the top. Blackface then, as agreed upon, began to beat at the door, but being flushed with drink, instead of entreating for an entrance, he shouted out to the serving-man, bidding him with many terrible oaths to come down and to render up his keys, for that they were come to relieve him of his charge.

'In the name of God, my masters,' cried the serving-man from the window, 'what do you want here?'

'We are come,' returned Blackface, 'to relieve you of your trust, so throw us down your keys.'

'An that be all,' said the serving-man, whose name was Adams, 'wait but a little while and you shall have the keys and my place to boot. Come again but a few hours hence, and you shall find me dead, when you may do with me and my trust as you list.'

'Come, come,' cries Blackface, 'no preaching, but come down and open, or we will bring fire and faggot to the door.'

'Ye shall not need,' answered Adams, 'hearken only to what I say, and you shall have free passage; but I give you fair warning, though I be but a single man, and without weapon, and sick even unto death, yet shall your coming in cost you as many lives as ye bear amongst you, for within these walls there is a dismal giant that hath slain his thousands, even the plague.' At these dreary words the courage of the robbers was taken somewhat aback, but Blackface spirited them on, saying it was no doubt an invention to deter them from the spoil.

'Alas,' answered Adams, who overheard their argument, 'what I say is the solemn and sorrowful truth, and which I am speaking for the last time, for I shall never see to-morrow's blessed sun. As for the door, I will open it to you with my own hands, beseeching you for your own sakes to stand a little apart, and out of the taint of my breath, which is sure destruction. There is one child herein a dead corpse, as you shall behold if you have so much courage, for it lieth unburied in the hall.' So saying he descended, and presently flung open the hall door, the villains withdrawing a little backward, and they saw verily by the light of a rush wick which he carried, that he was lapt only in a white sheet, and looking very pale and ghost-like, with a most dismal black circle round each of his eyes.

'If ye disbelieve me still,' he said, 'look inwards when I draw back from the door, and ye shall see what was a living child this day, but is now a corpse hastening to corruption. Alas! in the midst of life we are in death: she was seized at play.' With these words he drew aside, and the robbers looking through the door, perceived it was even as he said, for the dead body of the child was lying on the hall table, with the same black ring round its eyes, and dressed in brocade and riband as though death had carried it off, even as he said, in its holiday clothes. 'Now,' said Adams, after they had gazed awhile, 'here be the keys,' therewithal casting towards them a huge bunch; but the villains would now no more meddle with them than with so many aspics or scorpions, looking on them in truth as the very keys of death's door. Accordingly, after venting a few curses on their ill luck, they began to depart in very ill humour, when Adams again called to them to hear his last words.

'Now,' said he, 'though ye came hither with robbery, and perchance murder in your hearts, against me, yet as a true Christian will I not only forgive your wicked intents, but advise you how to shun that miserable end which my own life is coming to so very suddenly. Although your souls have been saved from sin, yet, doubtless ye have not stood so long in this infected air without peril to the health of your bodies, wherefore, by the advice of a dying man, go straightway from this over to Laytonstone, where there be tan pits, and sit there for a good hour amidst the strong smell of the tan, and which hath more virtue as a remedy against the infection of the plague, than even tobacco or the odour of drugs. Do this and live, for the poison is strong and subtle, and seizeth, ere one can be aware, on the springs of life.' Thereupon he uttered a dismal groan, and began yelling so fearfully that the robbers with one accord took to flight, and never stopped till they were come to Laytonstone, and into the tanner's very yard, where they sat down and stooped over the pit, snuffing up the odours with all the relish of men in whose nostrils it was as the breath of life. In which posture they had been sitting half an hour, when there entered several persons with a lantern, and which they took to be the tanner and his men, and to whom, therefore, they addressed themselves, begging pardon for their boldness, and entreating leave to continue awhile in the tan-yard to disinfect themselves of the plague; but they had hardly uttered these words, when lo! each man was suddenly seized upon, and bound in a twinkling, the constables, for such they were, jeering them withal, and saying the plague had been too busy to come itself, but had sent them a gallows and a halter instead, which would serve their turn. Whereupon, most of the rogues became very chop-fallen, but Blackface swore he could die easy but for one thing upon his mind, and that was, what had become of the dead child and the man dying of the plague, both of which he had seen with his own eyes. Hereupon, the man with a lantern turned the light upon his own face, which the rogues knew directly to be the countenance of Adams himself, but without any of those black rings round the eyes, and for which he explained he had been indebted to a little charcoal. 'As for the dead child,' he said, 'you must enquire, my masters, of the worshipful company of Barber Surgeons, and they will tell you of a certain waxen puppet of Hygeia, the Goddess of Health, which used to be carried at their pageants, and when it fell into disuse was purchased of them by my Lady Dame Ellinor Wood, for a plaything to her own children. So one head you see is worth four pair of hands, and your whole gang, tall, and strong knaves though you be, have been overmatched by one old man and a doll.'

Edgar Allan Poe's Plagues

Edgar Allan Poe (1809–49) was born in Boston, Massachusetts to working-class parents. His mother died when he was young and his father abandoned him, after which he was raised by foster-parents in Richmond, Virginia. He went on to serve in the US army at the age of 18 and, during this time, published his first book. When he was discharged, he pursued a literary career and wrote several short stories and newspaper articles. Much of his fiction was macabre, and he used the theme of plague in two literary works: *King Pest* and *The Mask of the Red Death. King Pest* is set during the time of the Black Death.[22] Infused with black humour, the story is a critique on the nature of power and on governments who, having shut off parts of London due to a plague epidemic, have let King Pest exert his dominion over the areas that are under a form of lockdown. Scarcely any introduction is needed for the *Mask of the Red Death* (later versions used 'Masque' in the title) which is one of Poe's most famous short stories. Originally published in *Graham's Magazine*, the story tells of a despotic Italian prince named Prospero who, seeing the plague decimate his land but unconcerned with the plight of his people, shuts himself away in a castle with members of his aristocratic court. Thinking that he and his nobles are safe from the disease, Prospero holds a masquerade in which there is feasting, and where the nobles present indulge in every kind of vice. Yet among the guests on this night a strange figure, clad in red, stalks the castle rooms and galleries – no one is safe from the disease for that figure is the personification of the Red Death![23]

From 'King Pest: A Tale Containing an Allegory' by Edgar Allan Poe (1835)

> The gods do bear and will allow in kings
> The things which they abhor in rascal routes.
> – *Buckhurst's Tragedy of Ferrex and Porrex.*

About twelve o'clock, one night in the month of August, and during the chivalrous reign of the third Edward, two seamen belonging to the crew of the *Free and Easy*, a trading schooner plying between Sluys and the Thames, and then at anchor in that river, were much astonished to find themselves seated in the tap-room of an ale-house in the parish of St. Andrews, London – which ale-house bore for sign the portraiture of a 'Jolly Tar.'

The room, although ill-contrived, smoke-blackened, low-pitched, and in every other respect agreeing with the general character of such places at the period – was, nevertheless, in the opinion of the grotesque groups scattered here and there within it, sufficiently well adapted to its purpose.

Of these groups our two seamen formed, I think, the most interesting, if not the most conspicuous.

The one who appeared to be the elder, and whom his companion addressed by the characteristic appellation of 'Legs,' was at the same time much the taller of the two. He might have measured six feet and a half, and an habitual stoop in the shoulders seemed to have been the necessary consequence of an altitude so enormous. Superfluities in height were, however, more than accounted for by deficiencies in other respects. He was exceedingly thin; and might, as his associates asserted, have answered, when drunk, for a pennant at the mast-head, or, when sober, have served for a jib-boom. But these jests, and others of a similar nature, had evidently produced, at no time, any effect upon the cachinnatory muscles of the tar. With high cheek-bones, a large hawk-nose, retreating chin, fallen under-jaw, and huge protruding white eyes, the expression of his countenance, although tinged with a species of dogged indifference to matters and things in general, was not the less utterly solemn and serious beyond all attempts at imitation or description.

The younger seaman was, in all outward appearance, the converse of his companion. His stature could not have exceeded four feet. A pair of stumpy bow-legs supported his squat, unwieldy figure, while his unusually short and thick arms, with no ordinary fists at their extremities, swung off dangling from his sides like the fins of a sea-turtle. Small eyes, of no particular color, twinkled far back in his head. His nose remained buried in the mass of flesh which enveloped his round, full, and purple face; and his thick upper-lip rested upon the still thicker one beneath with an air of complacent self-satisfaction, much heightened by the owner's habit of licking them at intervals. He evidently regarded his tall shipmate with a feeling half-wondrous, half-quizzical; and stared up occasionally in his face as the red setting sun stares up at the crags of Ben Nevis.

Various and eventful, however, had been the peregrinations of the worthy couple in and about the different tap-houses of the neighbourhood during the earlier hours of the night. Funds even the most ample, are not always everlasting: and it was with empty pockets our friends had ventured upon the present hostelrie.

At the precise period, then, when this history properly commences, Legs, and his fellow Hugh Tarpaulin, sat, each with both elbows resting upon the large oaken table in the middle of the floor, and with a hand upon either cheek. They were eyeing, from behind a huge flagon of unpaid-for 'humming-stuff,' the portentous words, 'No Chalk,' which to their indignation and astonishment were scored over the doorway by means of that very mineral whose presence they purported to deny. Not that the gift of decyphering written characters – a gift among the commonalty of that day considered little less cabalistical than the art of inditing – could, in strict justice, have been laid to the charge of either disciple of the sea; but there was, to say the truth, a certain twist in the formation of the letters – an indescribable lee-lurch about the whole – which foreboded, in the opinion of both seamen, a long run of dirty weather; and determined them at once, in the allegorical words of Legs himself, to 'pump ship, clew up all sail, and scud before the wind.'

Having accordingly disposed of what remained of the ale, and looped up the points of their short doublets, they finally made a bolt for the street. Although Tarpaulin rolled twice into the fire-place, mistaking it for the door, yet their escape was at length happily effected – and half after twelve o'clock found our heroes ripe for mischief, and running for life down a dark alley in the direction of St. Andrew's Stair, hotly pursued by the landlady of the 'Jolly Tar.'

At the epoch of this eventful tale, and periodically, for many years before and after, all England, but more especially the metropolis, resounded with the fearful cry of 'Plague!' The city was in a great measure depopulated – and in those horrible regions, in the vicinity of the Thames, where amid the dark, narrow, and filthy lanes and alleys, the Demon of Disease was supposed to have had his nativity, Awe, Terror, and Superstition were alone to be found stalking abroad.

By authority of the king such districts were placed under ban, and all persons forbidden, under pain of death, to intrude upon their dismal solitude. Yet neither the mandate of the monarch, nor the huge barriers erected at the entrances of the streets, nor the prospect of that loathsome death which, with almost absolute certainty, overwhelmed the wretch whom no peril could deter from the adventure, prevented the unfurnished and untenanted dwellings from being stripped, by the hand of nightly rapine, of every article, such as iron, brass, or lead-work, which could in any manner be turned to a profitable account.

Above all, it was usually found, upon the annual winter opening of the barriers, that locks, bolts, and secret cellars, had proved but slender protection to those rich stores of wines and liquors which, in consideration of the risk and trouble of removal, many of the numerous dealers having shops in the neighbourhood had consented to trust, during the period of exile, to so insufficient a security.

But there were very few of the terror-stricken people who attributed these doings to the agency of human hands. Pest-spirits, plague-goblins, and fever-demons, were the popular imps of mischief; and tales so blood-chilling were hourly told, that the whole mass of forbidden buildings was, at length, enveloped in terror as in a shroud, and the plunderer himself was often scared away by the horrors his own depreciations had created; leaving the entire vast circuit of prohibited district to gloom, silence, pestilence, and death.

It was by one of the terrific barriers already mentioned, and which indicated the region beyond to be under the Pest-ban, that, in scrambling down an alley, Legs and the worthy Hugh Tarpaulin found their progress suddenly impeded. To return was out of the question, and no time was to be lost, as their pursuers were close upon their heels. With thorough-bred seamen to clamber up the roughly fashioned plank-work was a trifle; and, maddened with the twofold excitement of exercise and liquor, they leaped unhesitatingly down within the enclosure, and holding on their drunken course with shouts and yellings, were soon bewildered in its noisome and intricate recesses.

Had they not, indeed, been intoxicated beyond moral sense, their reeling footsteps must have been palsied by the horrors of their situation. The air was cold and misty. The paving-stones, loosened from their beds, lay in wild disorder amid the tall, rank grass, which sprang up around the feet and ankles. Fallen houses choked up the streets. The most fetid and poisonous smells everywhere prevailed; – and by the aid of that ghastly light which, even at midnight, never fails to emanate from a vapory and pestilential atmosphere, might be discerned lying in the by-paths and alleys, or rotting in the windowless habitations, the carcass of many a nocturnal plunderer arrested by the hand of the plague in the very perpetration of his robbery.

But it lay not in the power of images, or sensations, or impediments such as these, to stay the course of men who, naturally brave, and at that time especially, brimful of courage and of 'humming-stuff,' would have reeled, as straight as their condition might have permitted, undauntedly into the very jaws of Death. Onward – still onward stalked the grim Legs, making the desolate solemnity echo and re-echo with yells like the terrific war-whoop of the Indian; and onward, still onward rolled the dumpy Tarpaulin, hanging on to the doublet of his more active companion, and far surpassing the latter's most strenuous exertions in the way of vocal music, by bull-roarings *in basso*, from the profundity of his stentorian lungs.

They had now evidently reached the strong hold of the pestilence. Their way at every step or plunge grew more noisome and more horrible – the paths more narrow and more intricate. Huge stones and beams falling momently from the decaying roofs above them, gave evidence, by their sullen and heavy descent, of the vast height of the surrounding houses; and while actual exertion became necessary to force a passage through frequent heaps of rubbish, it was by no means seldom that the hand fell upon a skeleton or rested upon a more fleshly corpse.

Suddenly, as the seamen stumbled against the entrance of a tall and ghastly-looking building, a yell more than usually shrill from the throat of the excited Legs, was replied to from within, in a rapid succession of wild, laughter-like, and fiendish shrieks. Nothing daunted at sounds which, of such a nature, at such a time, and in such a place, might have curdled the very blood in hearts less irrevocably on fire, the drunken couple rushed headlong against the door, burst it open, and staggered into the midst of things with a volley of curses.

The room within which they found themselves proved to be the shop of an undertaker; but an open trap-door, in a corner of the floor near the entrance, looked down upon a long range of wine-cellars, whose depths the occasional sound of bursting bottles proclaimed to be well stored with their appropriate contents. In the middle of the room stood a table – in the centre of which again arose a huge tub of what appeared to be punch. Bottles of various wines and cordials, together with jugs, pitchers, and flagons of every shape and quality, were scattered profusely upon the board. Around it, upon coffin-tressels, was seated a company of six. This company I will endeavor to delineate one by one.

Fronting the entrance, and elevated a little above his companions, sat a personage who appeared to be the president of the table. His stature was gaunt and tall, and Legs was confounded to behold in him a figure more emaciated than himself. His face was as yellow as saffron – but no feature excepting one alone, was sufficiently marked to merit a particular description. This one consisted in a forehead so unusually and hideously lofty, as to have the appearance of a bonnet or crown of flesh superadded upon the natural head. His mouth was puckered and dimpled into an expression of ghastly affability, and his eyes, as indeed the eyes of all at table, were glazed over with the fumes of intoxication. This gentleman was clothed from head to foot in a richly-embroidered black silk-velvet pall, wrapped negligently around his form after the fashion of a Spanish cloak. His head was stuck full of sable hearse-plumes, which he nodded to and fro with a jaunty and knowing air; and, in his right hand, he held a huge human thigh-bone, with which he appeared to have been just knocking down some member of the company for a song.

Opposite him, and with her back to the door, was a lady of no whit the less extraordinary character. Although quite as tall as the person just described, she had no right to complain of his unnatural emaciation. She was evidently in the last stage of a dropsy; and her figure resembled nearly that of the huge puncheon of October beer which stood, with the head driven in, close by her side, in a corner of the chamber. Her face was exceedingly round, red, and full; and the same peculiarity, or rather want of peculiarity, attached itself to her countenance, which I before mentioned in the case of the president – that is to say, only one feature of her face was sufficiently distinguished to need a separate characterization: indeed the acute Tarpaulin immediately observed that the same remark might have applied to each individual person of the party; every one of whom seemed to possess a monopoly of some particular portion of physiognomy. With the lady in question this portion proved to be the mouth. Commencing at the right ear, it swept with a terrific chasm to the left – the short pendants which she wore in either auricle continually bobbing into the aperture. She made, however, every exertion to keep her mouth closed and look dignified, in a dress consisting of a newly starched and ironed shroud coming up close under her chin, with a crimpled ruffle of cambric muslin.

At her right hand sat a diminutive young lady whom she appeared to patronise. This delicate little creature, in the trembling of her wasted fingers, in the livid hue of her lips, and in the slight hectic spot which tinged her otherwise leaden complexion, gave evident indications of a galloping consumption. An air of extreme *haut ton*, however, pervaded her whole appearance; she wore in a graceful and *dégagé* manner, a large and beautiful winding-sheet of the finest India lawn; her hair hung in ringlets over her neck; a soft smile played about her mouth; but her nose, extremely long, thin, sinuous, flexible and pimpled, hung down far below her under lip, and in spite of the delicate manner in which she now and then moved it to one side or the other with her tongue, gave to her countenance a somewhat equivocal expression.

Over against her, and upon the left of the dropsical lady, was seated a little puffy, wheezing, and gouty old man, whose cheeks reposed upon the shoulders of their owner, like two huge bladders of Oporto wine. With his arms folded, and with one bandaged leg deposited upon the table, he seemed to think himself entitled to some consideration. He evidently prided himself much upon every inch of his personal appearance, but took more especial delight in calling attention to his gaudy-colored surtout. This, to say the truth, must have cost him no little money, and was made to fit him exceedingly well – being fashioned from one of the curiously embroidered silken covers appertaining to those glorious escutcheons which, in England

and elsewhere, are customarily hung up, in some conspicuous place, upon the dwellings of departed aristocracy.

Next to him, and at the right hand of the president, was a gentleman in long white hose and cotton drawers. His frame shook, in a ridiculous manner, with a fit of what Tarpaulin called 'the horrors.' His jaws, which had been newly shaved, were tightly tied up by a bandage of muslin; and his arms being fastened in a similar way at the wrists, prevented him from helping himself too freely to the liquors upon the table; a precaution rendered necessary, in the opinion of Legs, by the peculiarly sottish and wine-bibbing cast of his visage. A pair of prodigious ears, nevertheless, which it was no doubt found impossible to confine, towered away into the atmosphere of the apartment, and were occasionally pricked up in a spasm, at the sound of the drawing of a cork.

Fronting him, sixthly and lastly, was situated a singularly stiff-looking personage, who, being afflicted with paralysis, must, to speak seriously, have felt very ill at ease in his unaccommodating habiliments. He was habited, somewhat uniquely, in a new and handsome mahogany coffin. Its top or head-piece pressed upon the skull of the wearer, and extended over it in the fashion of a hood, giving to the entire face an air of indescribable interest. Arm-holes had been cut in the sides, for the sake not more of elegance than of convenience; but the dress, nevertheless, prevented its proprietor from sitting as erect as his associates; and as he lay reclining against his tressel, at an angle of forty-five degrees, a pair of huge goggle eyes rolled up their awful whites towards the ceiling in absolute amazement at their own enormity.

Before each of the party lay a portion of a skull, which was used as a drinking cup. Overhead was suspended a human skeleton, by means of a rope tied round one of the legs and fastened to a ring in the ceiling. The other limb, confined by no such fetter, stuck off from the body at right angles, causing the whole loose and rattling frame to dangle and twirl about at the caprice of every occasional puff of wind which found its way into the apartment. In the cranium of this hideous thing lay quantity of ignited charcoal, which threw a fitful but vivid light over the entire scene; while coffins, and other wares appertaining to the shop of an undertaker, were piled high up around the room, and against the windows, preventing any ray from escaping into the street.

At sight of this extraordinary assembly, and of their still more extraordinary paraphernalia, our two seamen did not conduct themselves with that degree of decorum which might have been expected. Legs, leaning against the wall near which he happened to be standing, dropped his lower jaw still lower than usual, and spread open his eyes to their fullest extent: while Hugh Tarpaulin, stooping down so as to bring his nose upon a level with the table, and spreading out a palm upon either knee, burst into a long, loud, and obstreperous roar of very ill-timed and immoderate laughter.

Without, however, taking offence at behaviour so excessively rude, the tall president smiled very graciously upon the intruders – nodded to them in a dignified manner with his head of sable plumes – and, arising, took each by an arm, and led him to a seat which some others of the company had placed in the meantime for his accommodation. Legs to all this offered not the slightest resistance, but sat down as he was directed; while the gallant Hugh, removing his coffin tressel from its station near the head of the table, to the vicinity of the little consumptive lady in the winding sheet, plumped down by her side in high glee, and pouring out a skull of red wine, quaffed it to their better acquaintance. But at this presumption the stiff gentleman in the coffin seemed exceedingly nettled; and serious consequences might have ensued, had not the president, rapping upon the table with his truncheon, diverted the attention of all present to the following speech:

'It becomes our duty upon the present happy occasion – '

'Avast there!' interrupted Legs, looking very serious, 'avast there a bit, I say, and tell us who the devil ye all are, and what business ye have here, rigged off like the foul fiends, and swilling the snug blue ruin stowed away for the winter by my honest shipmate, Will Wimble, the undertaker!'

At this unpardonable piece of ill-breeding, all the original company half started to their feet, and uttered the same rapid succession of wild fiendish shrieks which had before caught the attention of the seamen. The president, however, was the first to recover his composure, and at length, turning to Legs with great dignity, recommenced:

'Most willingly will we gratify any reasonable curiosity on the part of guests so illustrious, unbidden though they be. Know then that in these dominions I am monarch, and here rule with undivided empire under the title of 'King Pest the First.'

'This apartment, which you no doubt profanely suppose to be the shop of Will Wimble the undertaker – a man whom we know not, and whose plebeian appellation has never before this night thwarted our royal ears – this apartment, I say, is the Dais-Chamber of our Palace, devoted to the councils of our kingdom, and to other sacred and lofty purposes.

'The noble lady who sits opposite is Queen Pest, our Serene Consort. The other exalted personages whom you behold are all of our family, and wear the insignia of the blood royal under the respective titles of 'His Grace the Arch Duke Pest-Iferous' – 'His Grace the Duke Pest-Ilential' – 'His Grace the Duke Tem-Pest' – and 'Her Serene Highness the Arch Duchess Ana-Pest.'

'As regards,' continued he, 'your demand of the business upon which we sit here in council, we might be pardoned for replying that it concerns, and concerns alone, our own private and regal interest, and is in no manner important to any other than ourself. But in consideration of those rights to which as guests and strangers you may feel yourselves entitled, we will furthermore explain that we are here this night, prepared by deep research and accurate investigation, to examine, analyze, and thoroughly determine the indefinable spirit – the incomprehensible qualities and nature – of those inestimable treasures of the palate, the wines, ales, and liqueurs of this goodly metropolis: by so doing to advance not more our own designs than the true welfare of that unearthly sovereign whose reign is over us all, whose dominions are unlimited, and whose name is 'Death'.'

'Whose name is Davy Jones!' ejaculated Tarpaulin, helping the lady by his side to a skull of liqueur, and pouring out a second for himself.

'Profane varlet!' said the president, now turning his attention to the worthy Hugh, 'profane and execrable wretch! – we have said, that in consideration of those rights which, even in thy filthy person, we feel no inclination to violate, we have condescended to make reply to thy rude and unseasonable inquiries. We nevertheless, for your unhallowed intrusion upon our councils, believe it our duty to mulct thee and thy companion in each a gallon of Black Strap – having imbibed which to the prosperity of our kingdom – at a single draught – and upon your bended knees – ye shall be forthwith free either to proceed upon your way, or remain and be admitted to the privileges of our table, according to your respective and individual pleasures.'

'It would be a matter of utter impossibility,' replied Legs, whom the assumptions and dignity of King Pest the First had evidently inspired some feelings of respect, and who arose and steadied himself by the table as he spoke – 'it would, please your majesty, be a matter of utter impossibility to stow away in my hold even one-fourth part of the same liquor which your majesty has just mentioned. To say nothing of the stuffs placed on board in the forenoon by way of ballast, and not to mention the various ales and liqueurs shipped this evening at different sea-ports, I have, at present, a full cargo of 'humming-stuff' taken in and duly paid for at the sign of the 'Jolly Tar.' You will, therefore, please your majesty, be so good as to take the will for the deed – for by no manner of means either can I or will I swallow another drop – least of all a drop of that villainous bilge-water that answers to the name of "Black Strap."'

'Belay that!' interrupted Tarpaulin, astonished not more at the length of his companion's speech than at the nature of his refusal – 'Belay that you lubber! – and I say, Legs, none of your palaver! *My* hull is still light, although I confess you yourself seem to be a little top-heavy; and as for the matter of your share of the cargo, why rather than raise a squall I would find stowage-room for it myself, but – '

'This proceeding,' interposed the president, 'is by no means in accordance with the terms of the mulct or sentence, which is in its nature Median, and not to be altered or recalled. The conditions we have imposed must be fulfilled to the letter, and that without a moment's hesitation – in failure of which fulfilment we decree that you do here be tied neck and heels together, and duly drowned as rebels in yon hogshead of October beer!'

'A sentence! – a sentence! – a righteous and just sentence! – a glorious decree! – a most worthy and upright, and holy condemnation!' shouted the Pest family altogether. The king elevated his forehead into innumerable wrinkles; the gouty little old man puffed like a pair of bellows; the lady of the winding sheet waved her nose to and fro; the gentleman in the cotton drawers pricked up his ears; she of the shroud gasped like a dying fish; and he of the coffin looked stiff and rolled up his eyes.

'Ugh! ugh! ugh!' chuckled Tarpaulin without heeding the general excitation, 'ugh! ugh! ugh! – ugh! ugh! ugh! – ugh! ugh! ugh! – I was saying,' said he, 'I was saying when Mr. King Pest poked in his marlin-spike, that as for the matter of two or three gallons more or less of Black Strap, it was a trifle to a tight sea-boat like myself not overstowed – but when it comes to drinking the health of the Devil (whom God assoilzie) and going down upon my marrow bones to his ill-favored majesty there, whom I know, as well as I know myself to be a sinner, to be nobody in the whole world, but Tim Hurlygurly the stage-player! – why! it's quite another guess sort of a thing, and utterly and altogether past my comprehension.'

The Greek historian Thucydides. (Public Domain Reproduction Licensed under Wikimedia Commons)

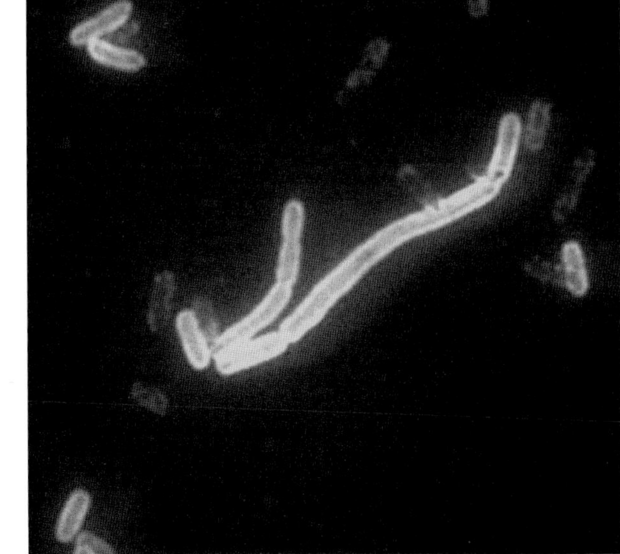

Plague (*Yersinia pestis*) under microscopy, dyed with fluorescent stain. Center for Disease Control and Prevention. (US Government public domain image)

Nicolas Poussin, *The Plague at Ashdod* (1631). Oil on canvas. Louvre, Paris. (Public Domain Reproduction Licensed under Wikimedia Commons)

Nicolas Poussin (1594–1655) was born in Normandy, France, and received a basic education before running away to Paris at the age of 18 to become an artist. Poussin's *The Plague at Ashdod* represents a scene from the First Book of Samuel. The Philistines, having captured the Israelites' Ark of the Covenant, are struck with plague. Bodies lay stretched in the streets; two figures carry a dead body while another figure sits listlessly on the Temple steps. The crumbling stone structure in the foreground symbolises the breakdown of the social order. Yet the means of the Philistines' salvation is close at hand; rats can be seen scuttling about and, to rid themselves of the plague, the Philistines will need to offer a sacrifice of the rodents.

Michiel Sweerts, *Plague in an Ancient City* (1652). Oil on canvas. Los Angeles County Museum of Art. (Public Domain Reproduction Licensed under Wikimedia Commons)

Michiel Sweerts (1618–64), a Flemish painter, spent the greater part of the 1640s in Rome, and witnessed an outbreak of plague in the city. The outbreak inspired him to paint *Plague in an Ancient City*. There are several haunting and thought-provoking images in the painting, such as the infant who struggles to nurse at its dead mother's breast. Adult figures are in a state of confusion; many women are bare-breasted while the male figures' clothes look shabby and torn.

Giovanni Boccaccio, author of *The Decameron*. (From Charles Sumner's *The Best Portraits in Engraving*, 1875)

Domenico Gargiulo, *Largo Mercatello a Napoli durante la peste del 1656*. Oil on canvas. Museo Nazionale di San Martino. (Public Domain Reproduction Licensed under Wikimedia Commons)

Domenico Gargiulo (1609–75) was born in Naples and studied art under the tutelage of the Neapolitan painter Aniello Falcone. Gargiulo specialised in landscapes and history paintings, as well as catastrophic events in his own era such as this depiction of the plague in Naples. There were periodic outbursts of bubonic plague in Italy during the seventeenth century; as is usual with seventeenth-century plague paintings, dead bodies lay in the street. In this picture, however, God looks on from above – does he feel sympathy for the plague victims? Has he caused the plague or is he simply indifferent?

Antoine-Jean Gros, *Bonaparte visitant les pestiférés de Jaffa* (1804). Oil on canvas. Louvre, Paris. (Public Domain Reproduction Licensed under Wikimedia Commons)

The French Siege of Jaffa (3–7 March 1799), was a decisive victory for Napoleon who entered the plague-stricken city on the last day. The artist Antoine-Jean Gros, who was one of Napoleon's cheerleaders, depicts Napoleon as statuesque and brave, fearlessly venturing into a veritable plague pit and helping the sick, thus combining the Enlightenment virtues of heroism and philanthropy.

Daniel Defoe. (Stephen Basdeo Personal Collection)

A

JOURNAL

OF THE

Plague Year:

BEING

Obſervations or Memorials,

Of the moſt Remarkable

OCCURRENCES,

As well

PUBLICK *as* PRIVATE,

Which happened in

L O N D O N

During the laſt

GREAT VISITATION

In 1665.

Written by a CITIZEN who continued all the while in *London*. Never made publick before

---

L O N D O N:

Printed for *E. Nutt* at the *Royal-Exchange*; *J. Roberts* in *Warwick-Lane*; *A. Dodd* without *Temple-Bar*; and *J. Graves* in St. *James's-ſtreet*. 1722.

Title page of Defoe's *Journal of the Plague Year* (1722). (Public Domain Reproduction Licensed under Wikimedia Commons)

William Harrison Ainsworth, author of *Old Saint Paul's* (1841). (Stephen Basdeo Personal Collection)

OLD SAINT PAUL'S.

BY WILLIAM HARRISON AINSWORTH.

BOOK THE FIRST.

APRIL, 1665.

CHAPTER I.

THE GROCER OF WOOD STREET AND HIS FAMILY.

ONE night, at the latter end of April, 1665, the family of a citizen of London, carrying on an extensive business as a grocer in Wood Street, Cheapside, were assembled, according to custom, at prayer. The grocer's name was Stephen Bloundel. His family consisted of his wife, three sons, and two daughters. He had, moreover, an apprentice; an elderly female serving as cook; her son, a young man about five-and-twenty, filling the place of porter to the shop and general assistant; and a kitchen-maid.

The whole household attended; for the worthy grocer, being a strict observer of his religious duties, as well as a rigid disciplinarian in other respects, suffered no one to be absent on any plea whatever, except indisposition, from morning and evening devotions; and these were always performed at stated times. In fact, the establishment was conducted with the regularity of clockwork, it being the aim of its master not to pass a single hour of the day unprofitably.

The ordinary prayers gone through, Stephen Bloundel offered up a long and fervent supplication to the Most High for protection against the devouring pestilence with which the city was then scourged. He acknowledged that this terrible visitation had been justly brought upon it by the wickedness of its inhabitants; that they deserved their doom, dreadful though it was; that, like the dwellers in Jerusalem before it was given up to ruin and desolation, they "had mocked the messengers of God and despised His word;" that, in the language of the prophet, "they had refused to hearken, and pulled away the shoulder, and stopped their ears that they should not hear; yea, had made their heart like an adamant stone, lest they should hear the law and the words which the Lord of Hosts had sent in His Spirit by the former prophets."

He admitted that great sins require great chastisement, and that the sins of London were enormous; that it was filled with strifes, seditions, heresies, murders, drunkenness, revellings, and every kind of abomination; that the ordinances of God were neglected, and all manner of vice openly practised; that, despite repeated warnings and afflictions less grievous than the present, these vicious practices had been persisted in.

All this he humbly acknowledged. But he implored a gracious Providence, in consideration of His few faithful servants, to spare the others yet a little longer, and give them a last chance of repentance and amendment; or, if this could not be, and their utter extirpation was inevitable, that the habitations of the devout might be exempted from the general destruction—might be places of refuge, as Zoar was to Lot.

He concluded by earnestly exhorting those around him to keep constant watch upon themselves; not to murmur at God's dealings and dispensations, but so to comport themselves, that "they might be able to stand in the day of wrath, in the day of death, and in the day of judgment." The exhortation produced a powerful effect upon its hearers, and they arose, some with serious, others with terrified, looks.

Before proceeding further, it may be desirable to show in what manner the dreadful pestilence referred to by the grocer commenced, and how far its ravages had already extended. Two years before—namely, in 1663—more than a third of the population of Amsterdam was carried off by a desolating plague. Hamburg was also grievously afflicted about the same time, and in the same manner.

Notwithstanding every effort to cut off communication with these states, the insidious disease found its way into England by means of some bales of merchandise, as it was suspected, at the latter end of the year 1664, when two persons died suddenly, with undoubted symptoms of the distemper, in Westminster. Its next appearance was at a house in Long Acre, and its victims two Frenchmen, who had brought goods from the Levant. Smothered for a short time, like a fire upon which coals had been heaped, it broke out with fresh fury in several places.

The consternation now began. The whole city was panic-stricken; nothing was talked of but the plague—nothing planned but means of arresting its progress—one grim and ghastly idea possessed the minds of all. Like a hideous phantom stalking the streets at noonday, and scaring all in its path, Death took his course through London, and selected his prey at pleasure.

The alarm was further increased by the predictions, confidently made, as to the vast numbers who would be swept away by the visitation; by the prognostications of astrologers; by the prophesyings of enthusiasts; by the denunciations of preachers, and by the portents and prodigies reported to have occurred.

During the long and frosty winter preceding this fatal year, a comet appeared in the heavens, the sickly colour of which was supposed to forebode the judgment about to follow. Blazing stars and other meteors, of a lurid hue and strange and preternatural shape, were likewise seen.

The sun was said to have set in streams of blood, and the moon to have shone without reflecting a shadow; grisly shapes appeared at night; strange clamours and groans were heard in the air; hearses, coffins, and heaps of unburied dead were discovered in the sky, and great cakes and clots of blood were found in the Tower moat; while a marvellous double tide occurred at London Bridge.

All these prodigies were currently reported, and in most cases believed.

The severe frost before noticed did not break up till the end of February, and with the thaw the plague frightfully increased in violence. From Drury Lane it spread along Holborn eastward as far as Great Turnstile, and westward to St. Giles's Pound, and so along the Tyburn Road. St. Andrew's, Holborn, was next infected; and as this was a much more populous parish than the former, the deaths were more numerous within it. For awhile the disease was checked by Fleet Ditch; it then leaped this narrow boundary, and ascending the opposite hill, carried fearful devastation into St. James's, Clerkenwell. At the same time it attacked St. Bride's, thinned the ranks of the thievish horde haunting Whitefriars, and proceeding in a westerly course, decimated St. Clement Danes.

Hitherto the city had escaped. The destroyer

DRINK THE PLAGUE! DRINK THE PLAGUE!

No. 1A.—XXIV.

Title page of the serialised John Dicks edition of Ainsworth's *Old Saint Paul's*. (Stephen Basdeo Personal Collection)

Edgar Allan Poe, pictured in June 1849 from a daguerreotype probably taken in June 1849 in Lowell, Massachusetts, photographer unknown. (Wikimedia Commons)

The personification of the Red Death illustrated by W.B. MacDougall for Margaret Armour's *The Eerie Book* in 1898. (Stephen Basdeo Personal Collection)

George W.M. Reynolds. (Stephen Basdeo Personal Collection)

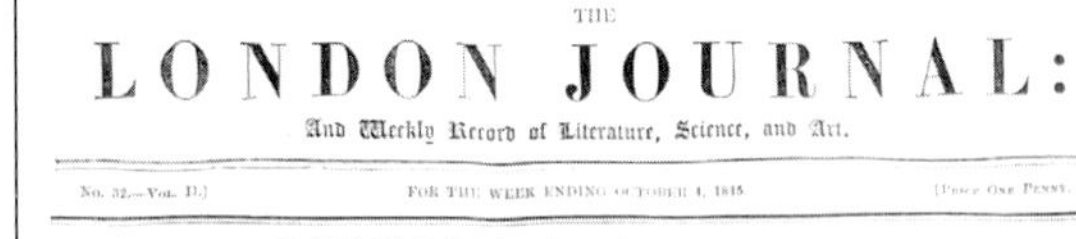

THE

LONDON JOURNAL:

And Weekly Record of Literature, Science, and Art.

No. 32.—Vol. II.] FOR THE WEEK ENDING OCTOBER 4, 1845. [Price One Penny.

[THE DEMON SHOWS THERESA TO FAUST.

FAUST.

BY GEORGE W. M. REYNOLDS.

Author of "The Mysteries of London," &c.

PROLOGUE.

It was the commencement of August, 1493.

The advance of rosy-fingered Morn had dispelled the clouds of darkness from the bosom of the Elbe, and the rays of the rising sun were reflected from the gilded pinnacles of the Castle-Church of Wittenberg.

On one side of the ancient town, from the banks of the river to the verge of a vast forest of pines, the luxuriant harvests waved their golden heads: on the other side the rich pasture-lands were covered with the flocks and herds of the Lord of Rosenthal.

But while the sun dawned on the fair scene, and the town, the University, the Castle, and the feudal mansion of Rosenthal, which stood on an adjacent hill, awoke to the light and bustle of a new day, it was still dark in the subterranean dungeons of the prison of Wittenberg.

Of all the wretched inmates of those drear abodes, none kept his eyes fixed upon the grated window of his solitary cell with more anxious longing than a youth in the unassuming garb of a student.

Seated on the straw in the corner of his lonely dungeon, he eagerly watched for the first beam that might deign to visit him.

For six long months had he pined in solitude in that cell—the deepest and darkest in the prison of Wittenberg.

Time had passed; but with the hours and days that dragged themselves along with such leaden feet, each fondly-cherished hope had departed from the student's breast.

Even his imagination—once so glowing and so enthusiastic in its visions—had at length failed to conjure up those phantoms which might make him believe that deliverance was near.

Yes—for six long months had he lingered in that dungeon, anxiously awaiting the hour which should enable him to justify himself before the criminal tribunal.

Six months had passed away in mingled hope and bitterness of heart; and he had prayed and wept, and wept and prayed by turns—how vainly!

Then he had shut his eyes, even in the midnight darkness of the dungeon, as if he could thus draw a veil over his maddening thoughts.

But still those thoughts haunted him in a thousand ghastly and appalling shapes, till he became afraid of the obscurity of his cell—hence his ardent longing for the presence of the sun.

What was that youth's crime?

He had loved—and still loved—a noble lady—dearly, madly loved her.

O Theresa! thine image seemed to smile at times amidst the gloom of his imprisonment, as the star from the midst of the thunder-clouds cheers the ocean-tossed mariner.

Yes—then he loved as fervently and well as ever man could love; and thy young heart beat with reciprocal tenderness for him.

But he was poor—a humble student; and Theresa was the only daughter and the heiress of the Lord of Rosenthal.

It was a crime in the haughty baron's eyes for one so low as the young student to aspire to the love of a maiden of such high degree; and by the influence of the vindictive father, the youth was thrown, on certain fictitious charges, into the prison of Wittenberg.

Such an atrocity was easily perpetrated in those times, when feudal power was predominant: and the same influence which had effected it had hitherto succeeded in delaying judicial investigation.

Thus the once noble and generous heart of that young man had been tutored by adversity and persecution to entertain and cherish sentiments of deadly vengeance against the powerful lord who had been the cause of his sufferings. Those sufferings were so intense that oft-times had he exclaimed, "Oh! that some power, celestial or infernal, would listen to my supplicating voice, and aid me in my misery! Fain would I give all hopes in this life for one hour of Theresa's love, and all my chances of heaven for one short minute of revenge!"

And these words he now repeated, for the thousandth time, as he sat upon his straw, watching for the appearance of the light.

Suddenly the bolts of his dungeon-door were drawn back, the heavy chain outside fell with a clanking din upon the stone floor, and the turnkey entered, bearing a lamp.

That light fell upon the handsome but care-worn features of the youth, whose chesnut hair, blue eyes, and fair complexion denoted him to be a true son of Saxon birth.

"What do you require of me?" exclaimed the student, starting from his straw pallet, and drawing up his noble and well knit form to its full height. "It is not the hour for my poor provender to be renewed: that duty you fulfil at night; and now, methinks, morning must be about to dawn. But, ah! perhaps you come to tell me that I am free," added the youth, his tone assuming a hasty expression of joy—"to announce to me the order for my liberation? Speak—is it so?"

And he clasped his hands together.

"Faust," returned the man, "in such a place as this one must be used to hear sad rather than happy tidings. It is for to-day!"

"To-day—my liberty!" ejaculated the young man

The first issue of G.W.M. Reynolds's *Faust: A Romance of the Secret Tribunals*, published in *The London Journal* in 1846. (Stephen Basdeo Personal Collection)

"VIENNA KNEW THAT THE PLAGUE HAD SEIZED UPON ITS VERY HEART!" (See p. 159.)

An illustration of the ravages of Mephistopheles' plague in Vienna, from Reynolds's *Faust*. (Stephen Basdeo Personal Collection)

Arnold Böcklin's *The Plague* (1898). Montana State University. (Wikimedia Commons)

Arnold Böcklin was a master of the macabre. Born in Basel, Switzerland, in 1827, he completed his training in various European cities. In 1898, he produced *The Plague* in which Death rides a bat-like creature whose breath kills all in its path.

THE LAST MAN.

BY

THE AUTHOR OF FRANKENSTEIN.

IN THREE VOLUMES.

Let no man seek
Henceforth to be foretold what shall befall
Him or his children.
MILTON.

VOL. I.

LONDON:
HENRY COLBURN, NEW BURLINGTON STREET.
1826.

Above left: The front cover of the first edition of *The Scarlet Plague* by Jack London. (Wikimedia Commons)

Above right: Title page of Mary Shelley's *The Last Man* (1826). (Wikimedia Commons)

A mural in Lisbon, Portugal, urges people to #STAYHOME during the Covid-19 pandemic. (Courtesy of Yohans Libot, via UnSplash)

Josse Lieferinxe, *Saint Sebastian Interceding for the Plague Stricken* (1497–99), Walters Art Museum. (Wikimedia Commons)

Saint Sebastian was a fourth-century Christian martyr. Europeans believed that praying to him could help to avert the onset of plague. Here, as a plague victim is buried, Sebastian, in heaven, intercedes on the victim's behalf.

The author Jack London, whose *The Scarlet Plague* (1912) can arguably be called the first 'modern' apocalypse story. (Wikimedia Commons)

Engraving of J. Delaunay's depiction of the Antonine Plague titled *The angel of death striking a door during the plague of Rome* (c.1800). (Wellcome Collection) Delaunay's depiction of the Antonine Plague sees Death descending on the streets of Ancient Rome.

Medieval Jews burned to death in Strasbourg on 14 February 1349. (Wikimedia Commons)

Plagues cause panic and, in a tale as old as time itself, people often blame foreigners and other marginalised populations for bringing plague with them. In Strasbourg, Jews were accused of starting the plague by poisoning the water wells. A particularly brutal aspect of this act of barbarity is the fact that Jewish babies who were thrown off the fire to escape being burned were thrown back in.

Michel Serre, *The Great Plague of Marseilles* (1720). (Wikimedia Commons)

The Great Plague of Marseilles in 1720 was the last major outbreak of bubonic plague in Western Europe. According to contemporary accounts, the plague arrived in the city when the merchant vessel *Grand-Saint-Antoine* docked at Marseilles with infected people on board. It is estimated that out of Marseilles' 90,000 strong population, approximately 50,000 died.

During the Great Plague of Marseilles, bubonic plague victims were hastily buried in mass graves. An excavation of these graves was carried out in the early 2000s, part of which can be seen in this photograph. (Wikimedia Commons)

The Resurrection Man and his Gang board a plague ship in search of plunder, from George W.M. Reynolds's *Mysteries of London* (1844–48). (Stephen Basdeo Personal Collection)

George W.M. Reynolds's *Mysteries of London* has some claim to being the biggest-selling novel of the nineteenth century. Full of intricate subplots featuring underworld characters, aristocratic villains and damsels in distress, the novel was published over four years in weekly instalments and was the soap opera of its day. Each issue featured an illustration and in this one, the sinister gang leader named the Resurrection Man, along with his gang, boards a plague ship. Placing merchant vessels in quarantine was a feature of port life in the early Victorian era, but the threat of the plague did not stop the likes of the Resurrection Man from boarding the ships in search of booty.

He was not allowed to finish this speech in tranquillity. At the name Tim Hurlygurly the whole assembly leaped from their name seats.

'Treason!' shouted his Majesty King Pest the First.

'Treason!' said the little man with the gout.

'Treason!' screamed the Arch Duchess Ana-Pest.

'Treason!' muttered the gentleman with his jaws tied up.

'Treason!' growled he of the coffin.

'Treason! treason!' shrieked her majesty of the mouth; and, seizing by the hinder part of his breeches the unfortunate Tarpaulin, who had just commenced pouring out for himself a skull of liqueur, she lifted him high into the air, and let him fall without ceremony into the huge open puncheon of his beloved ale. Bobbing up and down, for a few seconds, like an apple in a bowl of toddy, he, at length, finally disappeared amid the whirlpool of foam which, in the already effervescent liquor, his struggles easily succeeded in creating.

Not tamely, however, did the tall seaman behold the discomfiture of his companion. Jostling King Pest through the open trap, the valiant Legs slammed the door down upon him with an oath, and strode towards the centre of the room. Here tearing down the skeleton which swung over the table, he laid it about him with so much energy and good will, that, as the last glimpses of light died away within the apartment, he succeeded in knocking out the brains of the little gentleman with the gout. Rushing then with all his force against the fatal hogshead full of October ale and Hugh Tarpaulin, he rolled it over and over in an instant. Out burst a deluge of liquor so fierce – so impetuous – so overwhelming – that the room was flooded from wall to wall – the loaded table was overturned – the tressels were thrown upon their backs – the tub of punch into the fire-place – and the ladies into hysterics. Piles of death-furniture floundered about. Jugs, pitchers, and carboys mingled promiscuously in the *mêlée*, and wicker flagons encountered desperately with bottles of junk. The man with the horrors was drowned upon the spot – the little stiff gentleman floated off in his coffin – and the victorious Legs, seizing by the waist the fat lady in the shroud, rushed out with her into the street, and made a bee-line for the *Free and Easy*, followed under easy sail by the redoubtable Hugh Tarpaulin, who, having sneezed three or four times, panted and puffed after him with the Arch Duchess Ana-Pest.

From 'Mask of the Red Death' by Edgar Allan Poe (1842)

The 'Red Death' had long devastated the country. No pestilence had ever been so fatal, or so hideous. Blood was its Avatar and its seal – the redness and the horror of blood. There were sharp pains, and sudden dizziness, and then profuse bleeding at the pores, with dissolution. The scarlet stains upon the body and especially upon the face of the victim, were the pest ban which shut him out from the aid and from the sympathy of his fellow-men. And the whole seizure, progress and termination of the disease, were the incidents of half an hour.

But the Prince Prospero was happy and dauntless and sagacious. When his dominions were half depopulated, he summoned to his presence a thousand hale and light-hearted friends from among the knights and dames of his court, and with these retired to the deep seclusion of one of his castellated abbeys. This was an extensive and magnificent structure, the creation of the prince's own eccentric yet august taste. A strong and lofty wall girdled it in. This wall had gates of iron. The courtiers, having entered, brought furnaces and massy hammers and welded the bolts. They resolved to leave means neither of ingress nor egress to the sudden impulses of despair or of frenzy from within. The abbey was amply provisioned. With such precautions the courtiers might bid defiance to contagion. The external world could take care of itself. In the meantime it was folly to grieve, or to think. The prince had provided all the appliances of pleasure. There were buffoons, there were *improvisatori*, there were ballet-dancers, there were musicians, there was Beauty, there was wine. All these and security were within. Without was the 'Red Death'.

It was towards the close of the fifth or sixth month of his seclusion, and while the pestilence raged most furiously abroad, that the Prince Prospero entertained his thousand friends at a masked ball of the most unusual magnificence.

It was a voluptuous scene, that masquerade. But first let me tell of the rooms in which it was held. These were seven – an imperial suite. In many palaces, however, such suites form a long and straight vista, while the folding doors slide back nearly to the walls on either hand, so that the view of the whole extent is scarcely impeded. Here the case was very different, as might have been expected from the duke's love of the *bizarre*. The apartments were so irregularly disposed that the vision embraced but little more than one at a time. There was a sharp turn at every twenty or thirty yards, and at each turn a novel effect. To the right and left, in the middle of each wall, a tall and narrow Gothic window looked out upon a closed corridor which pursued the windings of the suite. These windows were of stained glass whose colour varied in accordance with the prevailing hue of the decorations of the chamber into which it opened. That at the eastern extremity was hung, for example in blue – and vividly blue were its windows. The second chamber was purple in its ornaments and tapestries, and here the panes were purple. The third was green throughout, and so were the casements. The fourth was furnished and lighted with orange – the fifth with white – the sixth with violet. The seventh apartment was closely shrouded in black velvet tapestries that hung all over the ceiling and down the walls, falling in heavy folds upon a carpet of the same material and hue. But in this chamber only, the colour of the windows failed to correspond with the decorations. The panes here were scarlet – a deep blood colour. Now in no one of the seven apartments was there any lamp or candelabrum, amid the profusion of golden ornaments that lay scattered to and fro or depended from the roof. There was no light of any kind emanating from lamp or candle within the suite of chambers. But in the corridors that followed the suite, there stood, opposite to each window, a heavy tripod, bearing a brazier of fire, that projected its rays through the tinted glass and so glaringly illumined the room. And thus were produced a multitude of gaudy and fantastic appearances. But in the western or black chamber the effect of the fire-light that streamed upon the dark hangings through the blood-tinted panes, was ghastly in the extreme, and produced so wild a look upon the countenances of those who entered, that there were few of the company bold enough to set foot within its precincts at all.

It was in this apartment, also, that there stood against the western wall, a gigantic clock of ebony. Its pendulum swung to and fro with a dull, heavy, monotonous clang; and when the minute-hand made the circuit of the face, and the hour was to be stricken, there came from the brazen lungs of the clock a sound which was clear and loud and deep and exceedingly musical, but of so peculiar a note and emphasis that, at each lapse of an hour, the musicians of the orchestra were constrained to pause, momentarily, in their performance, to harken to the sound; and thus the waltzers perforce ceased their evolutions; and there was a brief disconcert of the whole gay company; and, while the chimes of the clock yet rang, it was observed that the giddiest grew pale, and the more aged and sedate passed their hands over their brows as if in confused reverie or meditation. But when the echoes had fully ceased, a light laughter at once pervaded the assembly; the musicians looked at each other and smiled as if at their own nervousness and folly, and made whispering vows, each to the other, that the next chiming of the clock should produce in them no similar emotion; and then, after the lapse of sixty minutes, (which embrace three thousand and six hundred seconds of the Time that flies,) there came yet another chiming of the clock, and then were the same disconcert and tremulousness and meditation as before.

But, in spite of these things, it was a gay and magnificent revel. The tastes of the duke were peculiar. He had a fine eye for colours and effects. He disregarded the *decora* of mere fashion. His plans were bold and fiery, and his conceptions glowed with barbaric lustre. There are some who would have thought him mad. His followers felt that he was not. It was necessary to hear and see and touch him to be *sure* that he was not.

He had directed, in great part, the movable embellishments of the seven chambers, upon occasion of this great *fête*; and it was his own guiding taste which had given character to the masqueraders. Be sure they were grotesque. There were much glare and glitter and piquancy and phantasm – much of what has been since seen in 'Hernani'. There were arabesque figures with unsuited limbs and appointments. There were delirious fancies such as the madman fashions. There were much of the beautiful, much of the wanton, much of the *bizarre*, something of the terrible, and not a little of that which might have excited disgust. To and fro in the seven chambers there stalked, in fact, a multitude of dreams. And these – the dreams – writhed in and about taking hue from the rooms, and causing the wild music of the orchestra to seem as the echo of their steps. And, anon, there strikes the ebony clock which stands in the hall of the velvet. And then, for a moment, all is still, and all is silent save the voice of the clock. The dreams are stiff-frozen as they stand. But the echoes of the chime die away – they have endured but an instant – and a light, half-subdued laughter floats after them as they depart. And now again the music swells, and the dreams live, and writhe to and fro more merrily than ever, taking hue from the many tinted windows through which stream the rays from the tripods. But to the chamber which lies most westwardly of the seven, there are now none of the maskers who venture; for the night is waning away; and there flows a ruddier light through the blood-coloured panes; and the blackness of the sable drapery appals; and to him whose foot falls upon the sable carpet, there comes from the near clock of ebony a muffled peal more solemnly emphatic than any which reaches *their* ears who indulged in the more remote gaieties of the other apartments.

But these other apartments were densely crowded, and in them beat feverishly the heart of life. And the revel went whirlingly on, until at length there commenced the sounding of midnight upon the clock. And then the music ceased, as I have told; and the evolutions of the waltzers were quieted; and there was an uneasy cessation of all things as before. But now there were twelve strokes to be sounded by the bell of the clock; and thus it happened, perhaps, that more of thought crept, with more of time, into the meditations of the thoughtful among those who revelled. And thus too, it happened, perhaps, that before the last echoes of the last chime had utterly sunk into silence, there were many individuals in the crowd who had found leisure to become aware of the presence of a masked figure which had arrested the attention of no single individual before. And the rumour of this new presence having spread itself whisperingly around, there arose at length from the whole company a buzz, or murmur, expressive of disapprobation and surprise – then, finally, of terror, of horror, and of disgust.

In an assembly of phantasms such as I have painted, it may well be supposed that no ordinary appearance could have excited such sensation. In truth the masquerade licence of the night was nearly unlimited; but the figure in question had out-Heroded Herod, and gone beyond the bounds of even the prince's indefinite decorum. There are chords in the hearts of the most reckless which cannot be touched without emotion. Even with the utterly lost, to whom life and death are equally jests, there are matters of which no jest can be made. The whole company, indeed, seemed now deeply to feel that in the costume and bearing of the stranger neither wit nor propriety existed. The figure was tall and gaunt, and shrouded from head to foot in the habiliments of the grave. The mask which concealed the visage was made so nearly to resemble the countenance of a stiffened corpse that the closest scrutiny must have had difficulty in detecting the cheat. And yet all this might have been endured, if not approved, by the mad revellers around. But the mummer had gone so far as to assume the type of the Red Death. His vesture was dabbled in *blood* – and his broad brow, with all the features of the face, was besprinkled with the scarlet horror.

When the eyes of the Prince Prospero fell upon this spectral image (which, with a slow and solemn movement, as if more fully to sustain its role, stalked to and fro among the waltzers) he was seen to be convulsed, in the first moment with a strong shudder either of terror or distaste; but, in the next, his brow reddened with rage.

'Who dares,' – he demanded hoarsely of the courtiers who stood near him – 'who dares insult us with this blasphemous mockery? Seize him and unmask him – that we may know whom we have to hang, at sunrise, from the battlements!'

It was in the eastern or blue chamber in which stood the Prince Prospero as he uttered these words. They rang throughout the seven rooms loudly and clearly, for the prince was a bold and robust man, and the music had become hushed at the waving of his hand.

It was in the blue room where stood the prince, with a group of pale courtiers by his side. At first, as he spoke, there was a slight rushing movement of this group in the direction of the intruder, who at the moment was also near at hand, and now, with deliberate and stately step, made closer approach to the speaker. But from a certain nameless awe with which the mad assumptions of the mummer had inspired the whole party, there were found none who put forth hand to seize him; so that, unimpeded, he passed within a yard of the prince's person; and, while the vast assembly, as if with one impulse, shrank from the centres of the rooms to the walls, he made his way uninterruptedly, but with the same solemn and measured step which had distinguished him from the first, through the blue chamber to the purple – through the purple to the green – through the green to the orange – through this again to the white – and even thence to the violet, ere a decided movement had been made to arrest him. It was then, however, that the Prince Prospero, maddening with rage and the shame of his own momentary cowardice, rushed hurriedly through the six chambers, while none followed him on account of a deadly terror that had seized upon all. He bore aloft a drawn dagger, and had approached, in rapid impetuosity, to within three or four feet of the retreating figure, when the latter, having attained the extremity of the velvet apartment, turned suddenly and confronted his pursuer. There was a sharp cry – and the dagger dropped gleaming upon the sable carpet, upon which, instantly afterwards, fell prostrate in death the Prince Prospero. Then, summoning the wild courage of despair, a throng of the revellers at once threw themselves into the black apartment, and, seizing the mummer, whose tall figure stood erect and motionless within the shadow of the ebony clock, gasped in unutterable horror at finding the grave cerements and corpse-like mask, which they handled with so violent a rudeness, untenanted by any tangible form.

And now was acknowledged the presence of the Red Death. He had come like a thief in the night. And one by one dropped the revellers in the blood-bedewed halls of their revel, and died each in the despairing posture of his fall. And the life of the ebony clock went out with that of the last of the gay. And the flames of the tripods expired. And Darkness and Decay and the Red Death held illimitable dominion over all.

Mephistopheles, the Bringer of Pestilence

The following story is taken from G.W.M. Reynolds' novel *Faust: A Romance of the Secret Tribunals*, which was serialised in the *London Journal* between 1845 and 1846. Reynolds was of the most popular novelists of his day, being the author of several penny bloods and penny dreadfuls such as *The Mysteries of London* (1844–48). Reynolds also served as the editor for three highly popular newspapers and periodicals: *Reynolds's Miscellany*, *Reynolds's Political Instructor*, and the long-running *Reynolds's Weekly Newspaper* (1850–1967). Reynolds' *Faust* novel is based upon the centuries-old eponymous German folktale about a man who sells his soul to Satan to enjoy luxury and fame on earth for a limited period, after which demons drag him to Hell. Although a sympathetic character in adaptations written by the likes of Christopher Marlowe, in Reynolds' novel, Faust is a Gothic villain who often enjoys, through the exercise of his supernatural powers, harming the lives of other people. Having been wronged by the novel's hero, Count Otto of Vienna, Faust determines to punish the city and asks his demon-companion Mephistopheles to see it done. The Demon decides that he will bring a pestilence upon the city and Faust, unaware that Mephistopheles is planning a pestilence, watches in horror as miasmatic vapours envelop the Austrian capital.[24]

From *Faust: A Romance of the Secret Tribunals* by G.W.M. Reynolds (1845–46)

Almost at the same hour in the morning at which the confession and death of the physician took place at the house of Otto Pianalla, two tall forms stood on the summit of the Kalenberg, – that hill from which, nearly two centuries afterwards, the troops of Sobieski, King of Poland, rushed down upon the army of the Grand Vizier, Kara Mustapha, and delivered Vienna from the siege of the Ottomans.

Of those two persons, though both bore the human shape, yet only was human.

'Repeat thy wishes here,' said the Demon, in his deep sonorous voice, as he turned his eyes of supernal but sinister lustre upon Faust. 'It is not for me to search into thy motives: but I am ready to obey thy commands.'

'These, then, are my Wishes – these are my commands,' exclaimed Faust, who was in a state of extraordinary mental excitement: – 'by means of thine infernal power thou wilt perform some deed that shall avert the attention of Vienna from the everyday pursuits of life – that shall paralyse public affairs and private arrangements – that shall cause even lovers to forget their hopes of being immediately united at the altar!'

You command me to do a fearful thing, Faust,' said the Demon. 'Reflect for a moment – I would not have you reproach me hereafter!'

'I am decided – delay not, whatever be the consequences!' cried the Count, impatiently.

'One word ere the order go forth!' observed the Demon. 'Hast thou forgotten the whirlwind which I raised on the heights of the Brocken, and which devastated whole provinces in Germany?'

'I have forgotten nothing of all that,' answered Faust, 'and would that I could act now without recurrence to thy ferocious and infernal powers! But question me no farther – hesitate no longer! I care not what convulsion of nature – what awful visitation thou mayest bring about: only let not the result of thy command be temporary: – let it endure for weeks – ay, for months and months – so that it paralyse all the usual proceedings of society in this part of the world!'

'Thou shalt be obeyed!' cried the Demon.

Then, turning his face towards the East, he extended his right arm, and chanted the following incantation: –

'Come hither, fatal Cloud of Death!
O'er Europe roll with blasting breath;
Leave for awhile thy lov'd Japan;
Sweep o'er the heights of Kimengshan;
In Tartary, thou shalt not stay,
Nor rest o'er Persia in thy way:
Stop not on Ganges' bank to free
From funeral pyre the dark Suttee;
Let the Affghan unperill'd roam,
Nor pause to touch the Tartar's home;
Spare them that dwell upon the Nile;
Leave harmless each Ionian isle; –
But all thy power and fury bring
To Europe, on death-dealing wing:
Cover the land with corpse so'er
From Greece to Scandinavia's shore.
Let Turkey wail, and Russia groan,
And Italy give back the moan;
Let Germany thy presence know,
And France take up the tale of woe: –
Let not the lofty Pyrenees
From Spain ward off th'envenom'd breeze:
Rest on the Tagus for awhile, –
Then seek the Briton's sea-girt isle!'

When the Demon began to speak, Faust kept his eyes steadfastly fixed upon the East, towards which quarter the fiend addressed his terrible incantation. In a few minutes a thin vapour appeared to rise in the oriental horizon; and it gradually – gradually advanced towards Vienna – becoming every instant more palpable, and losing that transparency which was merely an appearance given to it by distance.

Onward it came – nearer and nearer, – expanding in volume – spreading itself out, with strange elasticity, over meadow, grove, village, town, plain, and hill, – – until it seemed one vast cloud, whose extremities touched the horizon on either side.

And onward – onward still it came; and now it approached the neighbourhood of Vienna – it swept over the Kalenberg, enveloping Faust and the Demon in a dense yellow mist.

But that mist! – how feculent was its odour – how nauseating the taste it created in the mouth – how oppressive its noxious density!

Faust trembled – he dared not ask the meaning of this strange and awe-inspiring visitation.

By the time the chant was concluded the mist had over spread the city and the country all around; and the air was as dark as if there was an eclipse of the sun.

The Demon's sonorous voice had ceased – and Faust beheld with appalling misgivings the first result of the incantation.

In a few moments the mist began to clear away from the eastern quarter: it was advancing westward – a huge and almost endless volume of dense and nauseating fog.

Onward still it went: by degrees it departed from all the territory which the eye could command east of the Kalenberg; and fast – fast it now rolled towards the west.

At length it began to diminish in bulk as it proceeded farther and farther in its course: again did it lose its appearance of denseness and its deep yellow hue – seeming more and more transparent as it receded towards the Atlantic.

From the moment that the incantation commenced until the mist appeared no larger than the palm of the hand in the western horizon, scarcely ten minutes had elapsed; – but those ten minutes appeared an age to the Count of Aurana.

'Fiend, what dread visitation is this?' he exclaimed, unable to endure any longer that torturing state of suspense.

'A visitation called forth in obedience to thy wishes,' answered the Demon, in a malignant tone of triumph; – 'a visitation evoked from the east, where it would have remained but for thy command!'

'And this visitation' cried Faust: 'what is it? What meant that horrible mist? what hast thou done to Vienna?'

'I have obeyed thee faithfully, Faust,' replied the Demon: 'society will now be paralysed indeed; – for the Plague is in Europe – the Black Death has already commenced its ravages in Vienna!'

'Fiend – demon! undo thine awful work!' exclaimed Faust, appalled at the terrible words which fell upon his ears.'

'No – it is too late!' answered the Demon calmly, 'did I not bid thee reflect? Blame not me! It is thou who hast done it all!'

And with folded arms he began to descend the mountain with slow and measured steps.

'Ah! wretch – monster that I am!' almost shrieked Faust, dashing his open palm against his forehead: – then, after a few moments' agonising hesitation, he rushed frantically down the hill, and entered the plague stricken city.

*

Yes: – fatal indeed was the incantation of the Demon – for the Black Death had suddenly manifested its terrible presence in Vienna!

When Faust re-entered the imperial city, he observed horror and dismay depicted upon the countenances of the inhabitants whom he met in the streets.

And those persons were not walking along with the usual appearance of security and confidence: – they were hurrying hither and thither, – pausing only to cross themselves at the doors of churches, or as they passed the niches in the walls where images of the saints were placed; then rushing wildly on until they reached the houses of the physicians of whom they were in quest.

Oh! how happy was he who found the medical attendant at home, and could prevail upon him to accompany him to his own house where a wife, a mother, a child, or other dear relative had suddenly been assailed by a pestilential malady!

And how horrible were the wailings of those who found no physicians disengaged, or who, having found them, vainly essayed prayers and threats to induce them to visit the plague-stricken victims!

For that dense cloud which had passed over Europe, was seen and even *felt* in Vienna, as elsewhere; and while it was still lingering over the city, men, women, and children were suddenly assailed with fearful symptoms, – struck down as it were by a flash of lightning that scared and scorched without killing them on the spot: – then, when the noxious mist had rolled away, rumour, with its myriad tongues, circulated from house to house, and street to street, the dread news how here and there those symptoms had appeared; – and in one short hour after the going forth of the infernal incantation from the heights of the Kalenberg, Vienna knew that the plague had seized upon its very heart!

And this plague, too, was of so malignant – so terrible a nature, that no other mortal scourge was known to possess such death-dealing influences. For, a hundred and sixty years before the period of which we are now writing, this same plague had ravaged Europe, and had carried off two-thirds of the entire population. Hence had that visitation received the terribly significant name of *the Great Mortality*, – and the pestilence itself was denominated with a not less fearful propriety, *the Black Death*.

Tradition had not allowed dumb oblivion to absorb one single detail of all the horrors that the first appearance of the Black Death, in the middle of the fourteenth century, had brought into Europe: – no – all the circumstances of that dread crusade of pestilential fury against human life had been duly preserved, and handed down from generation to generation; – and many, many a fervent prayer had been offered lip – many a princely fortune had been left to the Church to purchase masses – many a well-meaning but mistaken bigot had fled from the world and become an anchorite, – and all with the hope of moving heaven to save Christendom from another such visitation.

It was therefore with additional horror – with the wildest dismay – that Vienna now again recognised the presence of its terrible guest! At first, men were unwilling to believe that so awful an event could indeed recur: – they shrank aghast from even the idea of admitting that the Black Death could be again amongst them!

But as the symptoms, – those symptoms so well known by the traditionary memories of the former aspect and features of the dreadful malady, – developed themselves; – as farther reasoning against the possibility or even the probability of the return of the pestilence became the less feasible; – and as the awful conviction rapidly forced itself on the minds of those who had remained most obstinate in their scepticism, – then commenced scenes of a nature so appalling that no one can convey an idea of one tithe of their intense – their agonizing horror!

The ordinary pursuits of society were indeed paralysed; and all previously-formed plans of happiness, business, trade, occupation, and domestic arrangement, were checked as cruelly and abruptly as if every principle of the human mind were in a moment subverted.

Imagine a family party interrupted in the midst of its Christmas festivities by the sudden death of the master of the house as he sits at the head of his table: – what a fearful change is in a single instant brought into that dwelling! – how rapid is the transition there from joyous smiles to bitter tears – from peals of laughter to heart-breaking moans! Imagine this, we say – and it will give you, reader, some idea of the desolation and misery that abruptly seized upon the inhabitants of Vienna!

For when a pestilence enters the walls of a town, it produces a common wail, as if the entire people were only one vast family, and the town itself only one vast dwelling-house!

Brightly rose the sun that morning upon the imperial city; and the myriad inmates of those countless habitations awoke in the confidence of health and security. An hour passed – and how changed was the scene!

Death had entered the mighty capital with a two-edged scythe, and began to mow down the people on his right, and on his left, as if to fulfil the words of the inspired writer who solemnly said, 'ALL FLESH IS GRASS.'

And now, as Faust made his way through the streets, he beheld men running wildly along, and women, half-naked and with dishevelled hair, screaming from the casements and the balconies for aid.

The modest beauty which at other times would not have left its chamber without the lace covering upon the neck, now thought not of shame as it stood with bare bosom and naked arms at the door or the window, shrieking for a physician to hasten to a darling child, a dear husband, or a deeply-valued parent!

And shocking were the symptoms of this dire disease!

Inflammatory boils and tumours broke out upon the flesh with astounding rapidity; – the loveliest face was in one short half-hour rendered revolting with a putrid eruption; – and these blains speedily grew darker and more loathsome in hue, until they changed into the hideous black spots that gave to the pestilence its significant name.

Terrible pestilence!

Fearfully significant name!

Those black spots indicated a condition of putrid decomposition; – the tongue grew also black, and swelled so as nearly to suffocate the victim – lolling out of his parched mouth, and between his livid lips, and experiencing a thirst so burning that no beverage, however sharp or acid, could assuage that agonizing sensation: – large gouts of thick black blood were expectorated; – the breath exhaled an odour so nauseating that it was pestilence itself; – and violent pains crowned the infernal torments which the wretched patient thus endured.

Some – but these were a very few – ~became stupefied, lost their speech from palsy of the tongue, and sank into a lethargy which soon ended in death.

But by far the greater portion of the plague-stricken victims writhed on their beds, in horrible consciousness of their frightful state, – a consciousness to which the agony of pain and the heat of scorching thirst allowed no mitigation – no relief! Had they been encircled in the folds of a huge boa constrictor, – his coils twining tightly round their forms – his forked tongue licking their countenances – his pestiferous breath pouring with nauseous heat upon them – and the prospect of a horrible death from such a monstrous reptile before them, – they could not have suffered more!

All, save those few who fell into that lethargy which was so enviable in such a case, prayed that death would put a speedy end to their agonies; and many even laid violent hands upon themselves in the midst of their despair.

Contagious and infectious as it was, the Black Death proceeded not gradually with its ravages: its desolation was wholesale – vast – immense – unsparing throughout the imperial city.

The most sacred ties of kindred were in numerous cases utterly dissolved, – parents abandoning their infected children – children rushing in dismay from the houses where their parents lay writhing in the agonies of the plague – friends deserting dearest friends – husbands seeking a retreat from the pestilential breath of the wives whose beauty was late their pride and their joy – wives madly flying from the husbands whom they had erst pressed to their bosom – lovers turning in disgust, and loathing, and alarm from the mistresses adored an hour before!

The physicians themselves saw that human aid was vain, and that destruction inevitably awaited all who approached the infected.

Terrific mortality!

Appalling scourge of the human race.

And not only to the human race did its malignity extend; for its ravages were spread amongst the brute creation. If a dog touched the garments of a plague-stricken victim who fell dead or dying in the street, it caught the contagion – began to stagger about – and at length sank down and expired in horrid agonies, as if poison had been injected into its veins. The cat that sate on the domestic hearth escaped not the general desolation; and the bird that perched on the window-sill of the sick chamber, rose on buoyant wing no more.

From the diseased to the healthy – from the young to the old – from the old to the young – from man to the brute – and from the brute to man, spread the fury of the pestilence, as the flames in the prairies of the New World, extend from the dry grass to the withered tree, and over the heath, thence to the ripe corn, even unto the mighty forest, – streaming onward – onward, with a rage and a velocity which neither Indian nor animal can escape!

And such was the Black Death!

None who were seized with the terrible disease lived more than three days: some died in as many hours; – others fell dead upon the spot, as if struck with apoplexy or blasted by lightning; and, although they had not a spot upon their skin a moment previously, yet immediately afterwards their body was covered with the black plague boils.

The people of that age were inclined to superstitious belief, and a great majority were plunged in all the ignorance of bigotry: – – they were therefore easily accessible to absurd rumours and fanciful opinions. Moreover, the presence of such a fearful visitation prostrated all the mental energies of even those who escaped the contagion; and the most absurd, but alarming, reports prevailed.

Among other beliefs thus propagated, was one which obtained such general credence, and was of so appalling a nature, that it enhanced to a terrible degree the wild alarms naturally produced by the fury of the pestilence. It was believed, in a word, that the very eyes of the plague stricken were the sources of contagion; and thus the appealing glances which relatives turned towards relatives, and friends towards friends, when seized with the first dread warning of the malady, were deemed to be fiery arrows that would carry the venom of the Black Death to the hearts of all on whom those looks were cast.

But of what avail was flight to the timorous, since their garments were already saturated with the pestiferous atmosphere!

The End of the Human Race

The visionary writer Mary Shelley has a justifiable claim to have invented the genre of science fiction, notably with the publication of her novel *Frankenstein; or, The Modern Prometheus* (1818). *Frankenstein* was not her only novel, however, and Shelley went on to write several more works but which, upon their first publication, did not enjoy the success of her most famous tale. Yet in light of the Covid-19 pandemic in 2020, one of her later, forgotten novels came to public notice once more. This novel was *The Last Man*, published in three volumes by Henry Colburn in 1826. The novel begins in the year 2073 when the last English king, the enlightened Adrian, has abdicated and the country has become a republican commonwealth ruled by a lord protector. The first volume of the novel is rather philosophical, in which, through the medium of fiction, Shelley discusses several political, social and cultural questions. It is in the second volume that rumours of a plague in the East begin to surface. Like Shelley's associate Lord Byron, the former Lord Protector Raymond goes off to help fight the Greeks fight against the Turks. Accompanying Raymond is his wife, Perdita, who, although she would follow Raymond to the ends of the earth, is alarmed at the reports of a plague outbreak in Constantinople. Raymond rubbishes these reports and says that plague outbreaks are nothing new, especially in that part of the world. Raymond sadly dies in Greece, having enlisted to fight the Turks – just like Lord Byron – and Lionel Verney, the narrator and main protagonist who has also accompanied Raymond to Constantinople, brings her back to England. The plague, however, makes its way across the world killing all in its path and eventually arrives in England. Many of the motifs we find in modern-day apocalypse movies can be found in Shelley's novel: lawlessness and rioting, the rise of religious madmen, the hoarding of food, and scenes of desolate towns and cities. The extract presented here is a highly abridged one which provides an overview of how Shelley imagined the end of the world as ushered in by a pandemic. Towards the end of the novel, an extract of which is reproduced here, the plague has left only a handful of survivors in the whole of the United Kingdom. Lord Protector Adrian decides that the remaining citizens should travel to the continent to a more temperate climate where, they think, the plague will rage with less ferocity. With the exception of Lionel, all of the travellers die on the journey including Adrian, Lionel's wife Idris and Lionel's niece Clara. Eventually, only Lionel is left wandering the continent alone. He ventures to Rome and, reflecting on the fall of civilization (detailed in the extract below), realises that he is 'The Last Man' on earth.

From *The Last Man* by Mary Shelley (1826)[25]

I awoke in the morning, just as the higher windows of the lofty houses received the first beams of the rising sun. The birds were chirping, perched on the windows sills and deserted thresholds of the doors. I awoke, and my first thought was, Adrian and Clara are dead. I no longer shall be hailed by their good-morrow – or pass the long day in their society. I shall never see them more. The ocean has robbed me of them – stolen their hearts of love from their breasts, and given over to corruption what was dearer to me than light, or life, or hope.

I was an untaught shepherd-boy, when Adrian deigned to confer on me his friendship. The best years of my life had been passed with him. All I had possessed of this world's goods, of happiness, knowledge, or virtue – I owed to him. He had, in his person, his intellect, and rare qualities, given a glory to my life, which without him it had never known. Beyond all other beings he had taught me, that goodness, pure and single, can be an attribute of man. It was a sight for angels to congregate to behold, to view him lead, govern, and solace, the last days of the human race.

My lovely Clara also was lost to me – she who last of the daughters of man, exhibited all those feminine and maiden virtues, which poets, painters, and sculptors, have in their various languages strove to express. Yet, as far as she was concerned, could I lament that she was removed in early youth from the certain advent of misery? Pure she was of soul, and all her intents were holy. But her heart was the throne of love, and the sensibility her lovely countenance expressed, was the prophet of many woes, not the less deep and drear, because she would have for ever concealed them.

These two wondrously endowed beings had been spared from the universal wreck, to be my companions during the last year of solitude. I had felt, while they were with me, all their worth. I was conscious that every other sentiment, regret, or passion had by degrees merged into a yearning, clinging affection for them. I had not forgotten the sweet partner of my youth, mother of my children, my adored Idris; but I saw at least a part of her spirit alive again in her brother [Adrian]; and after, that by Evelyn's death [Evelyn was one of Lionel's children who died years ago] I had lost what most dearly recalled her to me; I enshrined her memory in Adrian's form, and endeavoured to confound the two dear ideas. I sound the depths of my heart, and try in vain to draw thence the expressions that can typify my love for these remnants of my race. If regret and sorrow came athwart me, as well it might in our solitary and uncertain state, the clear tones of Adrian's voice, and his fervent look, dissipated the gloom; or I was cheered unaware by the mild content and sweet resignation Clara's cloudless brow and deep blue eyes expressed. They were all to me – the suns of my benighted soul – repose in my weariness – slumber in my sleepless woe. Ill, most ill, with disjointed words, bare and weak, have I expressed the feeling with which I clung to them. I would have wound myself like ivy inextricably round them, so that the same blow might destroy us. I would have entered and been a part of them – so that

> If the dull substance of my flesh were thought,

even now I had accompanied them to their new and incommunicable abode.

Never shall I see them more. I am bereft of their dear converse – bereft of sight of them. I am a tree rent by lightning; never will the bark close over the bared fibres – never will their quivering life, torn by the winds, receive the opiate of a moment's balm. I am alone in the world – but that expression as yet was less pregnant with misery, than that Adrian and Clara are dead.

The tide of thought and feeling rolls on for ever the same, though the banks and shapes around, which govern its course, and the reflection in the wave, vary. Thus the sentiment of immediate loss in some sort decayed, while that of utter, irremediable loneliness grew on me with time. Three days I wandered through Ravenna – now thinking only of the beloved beings who slept in the oozy caves of ocean – now looking forward on the dread blank before me; shuddering to make an onward step – writhing at each change that marked the progress of the hours.

For three days I wandered to and fro in this melancholy town. I passed whole hours in going from house to house, listening whether I could detect some lurking sign of human existence. Sometimes I rang at a bell; it tinkled through the vaulted rooms, and silence succeeded to the sound. I called myself hopeless, yet still I hoped; and still disappointment ushered in the hours, intruding the cold, sharp steel which first pierced me, into the aching festering wound. I fed like a wild beast, which seizes its food only when stung by intolerable hunger. I did not change my garb, or seek the shelter of a roof, during all those days. Burning heats, nervous irritation, a ceaseless, but confused flow of thought, sleepless nights, and days instinct with a frenzy of agitation, possessed me during that time.

As the fever of my blood encreased, a desire of wandering came upon me. I remember, that the sun had set on the fifth day after my wreck, when, without purpose or aim, I quitted the town of Ravenna. I must have been very ill. Had I been possessed by more or less of delirium, that night had surely been my last; for, as I continued to walk on the banks of the Mantone, whose upward course I followed, I looked wistfully on the stream, acknowledging to myself that its pellucid waves could medicine my woes for ever, and was unable to account to myself for my tardiness in seeking their shelter from the poisoned arrows of thought, that were piercing me through and through. I walked a considerable part of the night, and excessive weariness at length conquered my repugnance to the availing myself of the deserted habitations of my species. The waning moon, which had just risen, shewed me a cottage, whose neat entrance and trim garden reminded me of my own England. I lifted up the latch of the door and entered. A kitchen first presented itself, where, guided by the moon beams, I found materials for striking a light. Within this was a bed room; the couch was furnished with sheets of snowy whiteness; the wood piled on the hearth, and an array as for a meal, might almost have deceived me into the dear belief that I had here found what I had so long sought – one survivor, a companion for my loneliness, a solace to my despair. I steeled myself against the delusion; the room itself was vacant: it was only prudent, I repeated to myself, to examine the rest of the house. I fancied that I was proof against the expectation; yet my heart beat audibly, as I laid my hand on the lock of each door, and it sunk again, when I perceived in each the same vacancy. Dark and silent they were as vaults; so I returned to the first chamber, wondering what sightless host had spread the materials for my repast, and my repose. I drew a chair to the table, and examined what the viands were of which I was to partake. In truth it was a death feast! The bread was blue and mouldy; the cheese lay a heap of dust. I did not dare examine the other dishes; a troop of ants passed in a double line across the table cloth; every utensil was covered with dust, with cobwebs, and myriads of dead flies: these were objects each and all betokening the fallaciousness of my expectations. Tears rushed into my eyes; surely this was a wanton display of the power of the destroyer. What had I done, that each sensitive nerve was thus to be anatomized? Yet why complain more now than ever? This vacant cottage revealed no new sorrow – the world was empty; mankind was dead – I knew it well – why quarrel therefore with an acknowledged and stale truth? Yet, as I said, I had hoped in the very heart of despair, so that every new impression of the hard-cut reality on my soul brought with it a fresh pang, telling me the yet unstudied lesson, that neither change of place nor time could bring alleviation to my misery, but that, as I now was, I must continue, day after day, month after month, year after year, while I lived. I hardly dared conjecture what space of time that expression implied. It is true, I was no longer in the first blush of manhood; neither had I declined far in the vale of years – men have accounted mine the prime of life: I had just entered my thirty-seventh year; every limb was as well knit, every articulation as true, as when I had acted the shepherd on the hills of Cumberland; and with these advantages I was to commence the train of solitary life. Such were the reflections that ushered in my slumber on that night.

The shelter, however, and less disturbed repose which I enjoyed, restored me the following morning to a greater portion of health and strength, than I had experienced since my fatal shipwreck. Among the stores I had discovered on searching the cottage the preceding night, was a quantity of dried grapes; these refreshed me in the morning, as I left my lodging and proceeded towards a town which I discerned at no great distance. As far as I could divine, it must have been Forli. I entered with pleasure its wide and grassy streets. All, it is true, pictured the excess of desolation; yet I loved to find myself in those spots which had been the abode of my fellow creatures. I delighted to traverse street after street, to look up at the tall houses, and repeat to myself, once they contained beings similar to myself – I was not always the wretch I am now. The wide square of Forli, the arcade around it, its light and pleasant aspect cheered me. I was pleased with the idea, that, if the earth should be again peopled, we, the lost race, would, in the relics left behind, present no contemptible exhibition of our powers to the new comers.

I entered one of the palaces, and opened the door of a magnificent saloon. I started – I looked again with renewed wonder. What wild-looking, unkempt, half-naked savage was that before me? The surprise was momentary.

I perceived that it was I myself whom I beheld in a large mirror at the end of the hall. No wonder that the lover of the princely Idris should fail to recognize himself in the miserable object there pourtrayed. My tattered dress was that in which I had crawled half alive from the tempestuous sea. My long and tangled hair hung in elf locks on my brow – my dark eyes, now hollow and wild, gleamed from under them – my cheeks were discoloured by the jaundice, which (the effect of misery and neglect) suffused my skin, and were half hid by a beard of many days' growth.

Yet why should I not remain thus, I thought; the world is dead, and this squalid attire is a fitter mourning garb than the foppery of a black suit. And thus, methinks, I should have remained, had not hope, without which I do not believe man could exist, whispered to me, that, in such a plight, I should be an object of fear and aversion to the being, preserved I knew not where, but I fondly trusted, at length, to be found by me. Will my readers scorn the vanity, that made me attire myself with some care, for the sake of this visionary being? Or will they forgive the freaks of a half crazed imagination? I can easily forgive myself – for hope, however vague, was so dear to me, and a sentiment of pleasure of so rare occurrence, that I yielded readily to any idea, that cherished the one, or promised any recurrence of the former to my sorrowing heart. After such occupation, I visited every street, alley, and nook of Forli. These Italian towns presented an appearance of still greater desolation, than those of England or

France. Plague had appeared here earlier – it had finished its course, and achieved its work much sooner than with us. Probably the last summer had found no human being alive, in all the track included between the shores of Calabria and the northern Alps. My search was utterly vain, yet I did not despond. Reason methought was on my side; and the chances were by no means contemptible, that there should exist in some part of Italy a survivor like myself – of a wasted, depopulate land. As therefore I rambled through the empty town, I formed my plan for future operations. I would continue to journey on towards Rome. After I should have satisfied myself, by a narrow search, that I left behind no human being in the towns through which I passed, I would write up in a conspicuous part of each, with white paint, in three languages, that 'Verney, the last of the race of Englishmen, had taken up his abode in Rome.'

In pursuance of this scheme, I entered a painter's shop, and procured myself the paint. It is strange that so trivial an occupation should have consoled, and even enlivened me. But grief renders one childish, despair fantastic. To this simple inscription, I merely added the adjuration, 'Friend, come! I wait for thee! – Deh, vieni! ti aspetto!' On the following morning, with something like hope for my companion, I quitted Forli on my way to Rome. Until now, agonizing retrospect, and dreary prospects for the future, had stung me when awake, and cradled me to my repose. Many times I had delivered myself up to the tyranny of anguish – many times I resolved a speedy end to my woes; and death by my own hands was a remedy, whose practicability was even cheering to me. What could I fear in the other world? If there were an hell, and I were doomed to it, I should come an adept to the sufferance of its tortures – the act were easy, the speedy and certain end of my deplorable tragedy. But now these thoughts faded before the new born expectation. I went on my way, not as before, feeling each hour, each minute, to be an age instinct with incalculable pain.

As I wandered along the plain, at the foot of the Appennines – through their vallies, and over their bleak summits, my path led me through a country which had been trodden by heroes, visited and admired by thousands. They had, as a tide, receded, leaving me blank and bare in the midst. But why complain? Did I not hope? – so I schooled myself, even after the enlivening spirit had really deserted me, and thus I was obliged to call up all the fortitude I could command, and that was not much, to prevent a recurrence of that chaotic and intolerable despair, that had succeeded to the miserable shipwreck, that had consummated every fear, and dashed to annihilation every joy.

I rose each day with the morning sun, and left my desolate inn. As my feet strayed through the unpeopled country, my thoughts rambled through the universe, and I was least miserable when I could, absorbed in reverie, forget the passage of the hours. Each evening, in spite of weariness, I detested to enter any dwelling, there to take up my nightly abode – I have sat, hour after hour, at the door of the cottage I had selected, unable to lift the latch, and meet face to face blank desertion within. Many nights, though autumnal mists were spread around, I passed under an ilex – many times I have supped on arbutus berries and chestnuts, making a fire, gypsy-like, on the ground – because wild natural scenery reminded me less acutely of my hopeless state of loneliness. I counted the days, and bore with me a peeled willow-wand, on which, as well as I could remember, I had notched the days that had elapsed since my wreck, and each night I added another unit to the melancholy sum.

I had toiled up a hill which led to Spoleto. Around was spread a plain, encircled by the chestnut-covered Appennines. A dark ravine was on one side, spanned by an aqueduct, whose tall arches were rooted in the dell below, and attested that man had once deigned to bestow labour and thought here, to adorn and civilize nature. Savage, ungrateful nature, which in wild sport defaced his remains, protruding her easily renewed, and fragile growth of wild flowers and parasite plants around his eternal edifices. I sat on a fragment of rock, and looked round. The sun had bathed in gold the western atmosphere, and in the east the clouds caught the radiance, and budded into transient loveliness. It set on a world that contained me alone for its inhabitant. I took out my wand – I counted the marks. Twenty-five were already traced – twenty-five days had already elapsed, since human voice had gladdened my ears, or human countenance met my gaze. Twenty-five long, weary days, succeeded by dark and lonesome nights, had mingled with foregone years, and had become a part of the past – the never to be recalled – a real, undeniable portion of my life – twenty-five long, long days.

Why this was not a month! – Why talk of days – or weeks – or months – I must grasp years in my imagination, if I would truly picture the future to myself – three, five, ten, twenty, fifty anniversaries of that fatal epoch might elapse – every year containing twelve months, each of more numerous calculation in a diary, than the twenty-five days gone by – Can it be? Will it be? – We had been used to look forward to death tremulously – wherefore, but because its place was obscure? But more terrible, and far more obscure, was the unveiled course of my lone futurity. I broke my wand; I threw it from me. I needed no recorder of the inch and barley-corn growth of my life, while my unquiet thoughts created other divisions, than those ruled over by the planets – and, in looking back on the age that had elapsed since I had been alone, I disdained to give the name of days and hours to the throes of agony which had in truth portioned it out.

I hid my face in my hands. The twitter of the young birds going to rest, and their rustling among the trees, disturbed the still evening-air – the crickets chirped – the aziolo cooed at intervals. My thoughts had been of death – these sounds spoke to me of life. I lifted up my eyes – a bat wheeled round – the sun had sunk behind the jagged line of mountains, and the paly, crescent moon was visible, silver white, amidst the orange sunset, and accompanied by one bright star, prolonged thus the twilight. A herd of cattle passed along in the dell below, untended, towards their watering place – the grass was rustled by a gentle breeze, and the olive-woods, mellowed into soft masses by the moonlight, contrasted their sea-green with the dark chestnut foliage. Yes, this is the earth; there is no change – no ruin – no rent made in her verdurous expanse; she continues to wheel round and round, with alternate night and day, through the sky, though man is not her adorner or inhabitant. Why could I not forget myself like one of those animals, and no longer suffer the wild tumult of misery that I endure? Yet, ah! what a deadly breach yawns between their state and mine! Have not they companions? Have not they each their mate – their cherished young, their home, which, though unexpressed to us, is, I doubt not, endeared and enriched, even in their eyes, by the society which kind nature has created for them? It is I only that am alone – I, on this little hill top, gazing on plain and mountain recess – on sky, and its starry population, listening to every sound of earth, and air, and murmuring wave, – I only cannot express to any companion my many thoughts, nor lay my throbbing head on any loved bosom, nor drink from meeting eyes an intoxicating dew, that transcends the fabulous nectar of the gods. Shall I not then complain? Shall I not curse the murderous engine which has mowed down the children of men, my brethren? Shall I not bestow a malediction on every other of nature's offspring, which dares live and enjoy, while I live and suffer?

Ah, no! I will discipline my sorrowing heart to sympathy in your joys; I will be happy, because ye are so. Live on, ye innocents, nature's selected darlings; I am not much unlike to you. Nerves, pulse, brain, joint, and flesh, of such am I composed, and ye are organized by the same laws. I have something beyond this, but I will call it a defect, not an endowment, if it leads me to misery, while ye are happy. Just then, there emerged from a near copse two goats and a little kid, by the mother's side; they began to browze the herbage of the hill. I approached near to them, without their perceiving me; I gathered a handful of fresh grass, and held it out; the little one nestled close to its mother, while she timidly withdrew. The male stepped forward, fixing his eyes on me: I drew near, still holding out my lure, while he, depressing his head, rushed at me with his horns. I was a very fool; I knew it, yet I yielded to my rage. I snatched up a huge fragment of rock; it would have crushed my rash foe. I poized it – aimed it – then my heart failed me. I hurled it wide of the mark; it rolled clattering among the bushes into dell. My little visitants, all aghast, galloped back into the covert of the wood; while I, my very heart bleeding and torn, rushed down the hill, and by the violence of bodily exertion, sought to escape from my miserable self.

No, no, I will not live among the wild scenes of nature, the enemy of all that lives. I will seek the towns – Rome, the capital of the world, the crown of man's achievements. Among its storied streets, hallowed ruins, and stupendous remains of human exertion, I shall not, as here, find every thing forgetful of man; trampling on his memory, defacing his works, proclaiming from hill to hill, and vale to vale, – by the torrents freed from the boundaries which he imposed – by the vegetation liberated from the laws which he enforced – by his habitation abandoned to mildew and weeds, that his power is lost, his race annihilated for ever.

I hailed the Tiber, for that was as it were an unalienable possession of humanity. I hailed the wild Campagna, for every rood had been trod by man; and its savage uncultivation, of no recent date, only proclaimed more distinctly his power, since he had given an honourable name and sacred title to what else would have been a worthless, barren track. I entered Eternal Rome by the Porta del Popolo, and saluted with awe its time-honoured space. The wide square, the churches near, the long extent of the Corso, the near eminence of Trinita de' Monti appeared like fairy work, they were so silent, so peaceful, and so very fair. It was evening; and the population of animals which still existed in this mighty city, had gone to rest; there was no sound, save the murmur of its many fountains, whose soft monotony was harmony to my soul. The knowledge that I was in Rome, soothed me; that wondrous city, hardly more illustrious for its heroes and sages, than for the power it exercised over the imaginations of men. I went to rest that night; the eternal burning of my heart quenched, – my senses tranquil.

The next morning I eagerly began my rambles in search of oblivion. I ascended the many terraces of the garden of the Colonna Palace, under whose roof I had been sleeping; and passing out from it at its summit, I found myself on Monte Cavallo. The fountain sparkled in the sun; the obelisk above pierced the clear dark-blue air. The statues on each side, the works, as they are inscribed, of Phidias and Praxiteles, stood in undiminished grandeur, representing Castor and Pollux, who with majestic power tamed the rearing animal at their side. If those illustrious artists had in truth chiselled these forms, how many passing generations had their giant proportions outlived! and now they were viewed by the last of the species they were sculptured to represent and deify. I had shrunk into insignificance in my own eyes, as I considered the multitudinous beings these stone demigods had outlived, but this after-thought restored me to dignity in my own conception. The sight of the poetry eternized in these statues, took the sting from the thought, arraying it only in poetic ideality.

I repeated to myself, – I am in Rome! I behold, and as it were, familiarly converse with the wonder of the world, sovereign mistress of the imagination, majestic and eternal survivor of millions of generations of extinct men. I endeavoured to quiet the sorrows of my aching heart, by even now taking an interest in what in my youth I had ardently longed to see. Every part of Rome is replete with relics of ancient times. The meanest streets are strewed with truncated columns, broken capitals – Corinthian and Ionic, and sparkling fragments of granite or porphyry. The walls of the most penurious dwellings enclose a fluted pillar or ponderous stone, which once made part of the palace of the Caesars; and the voice of dead time, in still vibrations, is breathed from these dumb things, animated and glorified as they were by man.

I embraced the vast columns of the temple of Jupiter Stator, which survives in the open space that was the Forum, and leaning my burning cheek against its cold durability, I tried to lose the sense of present misery and present desertion, by recalling to the haunted cell of my brain vivid memories of times gone by. I rejoiced at my success, as I figured Camillus, the Gracchi, Cato, and last the heroes of Tacitus, which shine meteors of surpassing brightness during the murky night of the empire; – as the verses of Horace and Virgil, or the glowing periods of Cicero thronged into the opened gates of my mind, I felt myself exalted by long forgotten enthusiasm. I was delighted to know that I beheld the scene which they beheld – the scene which their wives and mothers, and crowds of the unnamed witnessed, while at the same time they honoured, applauded, or wept for these matchless specimens of humanity. At length, then, I had found a consolation. I had not vainly sought the storied precincts of Rome – I had discovered a medicine for my many and vital wounds.

I sat at the foot of these vast columns. The Coliseum, whose naked ruin is robed by nature in a verdurous and glowing veil, lay in the sunlight on my right. Not far off, to the left, was the Tower of the Capitol. Triumphal arches, the falling walls of many temples, strewed the ground at my feet. I strove, I resolved, to force myself to see the Plebeian multitude and lofty Patrician forms congregated around; and, as the Diorama of ages passed across my subdued fancy, they were replaced by the modern Roman; the Pope, in his white stole, distributing benedictions to the kneeling worshippers; the friar in his cowl; the dark-eyed girl, veiled by her mezzera; the noisy, sun-burnt rustic, leading his herd of buffaloes and oxen to the Campo Vaccino. The romance with which, dipping our pencils in the rainbow hues of sky and transcendent nature, we to a degree gratuitously endow the Italians, replaced the solemn grandeur of antiquity. I remembered the dark monk, and floating figures of 'The Italian,' and how my boyish blood had thrilled at the description. I called to mind Corinna ascending the Capitol to be crowned, and, passing from the heroine to the author, reflected how the Enchantress Spirit of Rome held sovereign sway over the minds of the imaginative, until it rested on me – sole remaining spectator of its wonders.

I was long wrapt by such ideas; but the soul wearies of a pauseless flight; and, stooping from its wheeling circuits round and round this spot, suddenly it fell ten thousand fathom deep, into the abyss of the present – into self-knowledge – into tenfold sadness. I roused myself – I cast off my waking dreams; and I, who just now could almost hear the shouts of the Roman throng, and was hustled by countless multitudes, now beheld the desart ruins of Rome sleeping under its own blue sky; the shadows lay tranquilly on the ground; sheep were grazing untended on the Palatine, and a buffalo stalked down the Sacred Way that led to the Capitol. I was alone in the Forum; alone in Rome; alone in the world. Would not one living man – one companion in my weary solitude, be worth all the glory and remembered power of this time-honoured city? Double sorrow – sadness, bred in Cimmerian caves, robed my soul in a mourning garb. The generations I had conjured up to my fancy, contrasted more strongly with the end of all – the single point in which, as a pyramid, the mighty fabric of society had ended, while I, on the giddy height, saw vacant space around me.

From such vague laments I turned to the contemplation of the minutiae of my situation. So far, I had not succeeded in the sole object of my desires, the finding a companion for my desolation. Yet I did not despair. It is true that my inscriptions were set up for the most part, in insignificant towns and villages; yet, even without these memorials, it was possible that the person, who like me should find himself alone in a depopulate land, should, like me, come to Rome. The more slender my expectation was, the more I chose to build on it, and to accommodate my actions to this vague possibility.

It became necessary therefore, that for a time I should domesticate myself at Rome. It became necessary, that I should look my disaster in the face – not playing the school-boy's part of obedience without submission; enduring life, and yet rebelling against the laws by which I lived.

Yet how could I resign myself? Without love, without sympathy, without communion with any, how could I meet the morning sun, and with it trace its oft repeated journey to the evening shades? Why did I continue to live – why not throw off the weary weight of time, and with my own hand, let out the fluttering prisoner from my agonized breast? – It was not cowardice that withheld me; for the true fortitude was to endure; and death had a soothing sound accompanying it, that would easily entice me to enter its demesne. But this I would not do. I had, from the moment I had reasoned on the subject, instituted myself the subject to fate, and the servant of necessity, the visible laws of the invisible God – I believed that my obedience was the result of sound reasoning, pure feeling, and an exalted sense of the true excellence and nobility of my nature. Could I have seen in this empty earth, in the seasons and their change, the hand of a blind power only, most willingly would I have placed my head on the sod, and closed my eyes on its loveliness for ever. But fate had administered life to me, when the plague had already seized on its prey – she had dragged me by the hair from out the strangling waves – By such miracles she had bought me for her own; I admitted her authority, and bowed to her decrees. If, after mature consideration, such was my resolve, it was doubly necessary that I should not lose the end of life, the improvement of my faculties, and poison its flow by repinings without end. Yet how cease to repine, since there was no hand near to extract the barbed spear that had entered my heart of hearts? I stretched out my hand, and it touched none whose sensations were responsive to mine. I was girded, walled in, vaulted over, by seven-fold barriers of loneliness. Occupation alone, if I could deliver myself up to it, would be capable of affording an opiate to my sleepless sense of woe. Having determined to make Rome my abode, at least for some months, I made arrangements for my accommodation – I selected my home. The Colonna Palace was well adapted for my purpose. Its grandeur – its treasure of paintings, its magnificent halls were objects soothing and even exhilarating.

I found the granaries of Rome well stored with grain, and particularly with Indian corn; this product requiring less art in its preparation for food, I selected as my principal support. I now found the hardships and lawlessness of my youth turn to account. A man cannot throw off the habits of sixteen years. Since that age, it is true, I had lived luxuriously, or at least surrounded by all the conveniences civilization afforded. But before that time, I had been 'as uncouth a savage, as the wolf-bred founder of old Rome' – and now, in Rome itself, robber and shepherd propensities, similar to those of its founder, were of advantage to its sole inhabitant. I spent the morning riding and shooting in the Campagna – I passed long hours in the various galleries – I gazed at each statue, and lost myself in a reverie before many a fair Madonna or beauteous nymph. I haunted the Vatican, and stood surrounded by marble forms of divine beauty. Each stone deity was possessed by sacred gladness, and the eternal fruition of love. They looked on me with unsympathizing complacency, and often in wild accents I reproached them for their supreme indifference – for they were human shapes, the human form divine was manifest in each fairest limb and lineament. The perfect moulding brought with it the idea of colour and motion; often, half in bitter mockery, half in self-delusion, I clasped their icy proportions, and, coming between Cupid and his Psyche's lips, pressed the unconceiving marble.

I endeavoured to read. I visited the libraries of Rome. I selected a volume, and, choosing some sequestered, shady nook, on the banks of the Tiber, or opposite the fair temple in the Borghese Gardens, or under the old pyramid of Cestius, I endeavoured to conceal me from myself, and immerse myself in the subject traced on the pages before me. As if in the same soil you plant nightshade and a myrtle tree, they will each appropriate the mould, moisture, and air administered, for the fostering their several properties – so did my grief find sustenance, and power of existence, and growth, in what else had been divine manna, to feed radiant meditation. Ah! while I streak this paper with the tale of what my so named occupations were – while I shape the skeleton of my days – my hand trembles – my heart pants, and my brain refuses to lend expression, or phrase, or idea, by which to image forth the veil of unutterable woe that clothed these bare realities. O, worn and beating heart, may I dissect thy fibres, and tell how in each unmitigable misery, sadness dire, repinings, and despair, existed? May I record my many ravings – the wild curses I hurled at torturing nature – and how I have passed days shut out from light and food – from all except the burning hell alive in my own bosom?

I was presented, meantime, with one other occupation, the one best fitted to discipline my melancholy thoughts, which strayed backwards, over many a ruin, and through many a flowery glade, even to the mountain recess, from which in early youth I had first emerged.

During one of my rambles through the habitations of Rome, I found writing materials on a table in an author's study. Parts of a manuscript lay scattered about. It contained a learned disquisition on the Italian language; one page an unfinished dedication to posterity, for whose profit the writer had sifted and selected the niceties of this harmonious language – to whose everlasting benefit he bequeathed his labours.

I also will write a book, I cried – for whom to read? – to whom dedicated? And then with silly flourish (what so capricious and childish as despair?) I wrote, DEDICATION TO THE ILLUSTRIOUS DEAD. SHADOWS, ARISE, AND READ YOUR FALL! BEHOLD THE HISTORY OF THE LAST MAN.

Yet, will not this world be re-peopled, and the children of a saved pair of lovers, in some to me unknown and unattainable seclusion, wandering to these prodigious relics of the ante-pestilential race, seek to learn how beings so wondrous in their achievements, with imaginations infinite, and powers godlike, had departed from their home to an unknown country?

I will write and leave in this most ancient city, this 'world's sole monument,' a record of these things. I will leave a monument of the existence of Verney, the Last Man. At first I thought only to speak of plague, of death, and last, of desertion; but I lingered fondly on my early years, and recorded with sacred zeal the virtues of my companions. They have been with me during the fulfilment of my task. I have brought it to an end – I lift my eyes from my paper – again they are lost to me. Again I feel that I am alone.

A year has passed since I have been thus occupied. The seasons have made their wonted round, and decked this eternal city in a changeful robe of surpassing beauty. A year has passed; and I no longer guess at my state or my prospects – loneliness is my familiar, sorrow my inseparable companion. I have endeavoured to brave the storm – I have endeavoured to school myself to fortitude – I have sought to imbue myself with the lessons of wisdom. It will not do. My hair has become nearly grey – my voice, unused now to utter sound, comes strangely on my ears. My person, with its human powers and features, seem to me a monstrous excrescence of nature. How express in human language a woe human being until this hour never knew! How give intelligible expression to a pang none but I could ever understand! – No one has entered Rome. None will ever come. I smile bitterly at the delusion I have so long nourished, and still more, when I reflect that I have exchanged it for another as delusive, as false, but to which I now cling with the same fond trust.

Winter has come again; and the gardens of Rome have lost their leaves – the sharp air comes over the Campagna, and has driven its brute inhabitants to take up their abode in the many dwellings of the deserted city – frost has suspended the gushing fountains – and Trevi has stilled her eternal music. I had made a rough calculation, aided by the stars, by which I endeavoured to ascertain the first day of the new year. In the old out-worn age, the Sovereign Pontiff was used to go in solemn pomp, and mark the renewal of the year by driving a nail in the gate of the temple of Janus. On that day I ascended St. Peter's, and carved on its topmost stone the aera 2100, last year of the world!

My only companion was a dog, a shaggy fellow, half water and half shepherd's dog, whom I found tending sheep in the Campagna. His master was dead, but nevertheless he continued fulfilling his duties in expectation of his return. If a sheep strayed from the rest, he forced it to return to the flock, and sedulously kept off every intruder. Riding in the Campagna I had come upon his sheep-walk, and for some time observed his repetition of lessons learned from man, now useless, though unforgotten. His delight was excessive when he saw me. He sprung up to my knees; he capered round and round, wagging his tail, with the short, quick bark of pleasure: he left his fold to follow me, and from that day has never neglected to watch by and attend on me, shewing boisterous gratitude whenever I caressed or talked to him. His pattering steps and mine alone were heard, when we entered the magnificent extent of nave and aisle of St. Peter's. We ascended the myriad steps together, when on the summit I achieved my design, and in rough figures noted the date of the last year. I then turned to gaze on the country, and to take leave of Rome. I had long determined to quit it, and I now formed the plan I would adopt for my future career, after I had left this magnificent abode.

A solitary being is by instinct a wanderer, and that I would become. A hope of amelioration always attends on change of place, which would even lighten the burthen of my life. I had been a fool to remain in Rome all this time: Rome noted for Malaria, the famous caterer for death. But it was still possible, that, could I visit the whole extent of earth, I should find in some part of the wide extent a survivor. Methought the sea-side was the most probable retreat to be chosen by such a one. If left alone in an inland district, still they could not continue in the spot where their last hopes had been extinguished; they would journey on, like me, in search of a partner for their solitude, till the watery barrier stopped their further progress.

To that water – cause of my woes, perhaps now to be their cure, I would betake myself. Farewell, Italy! – farewell, thou ornament of the world, matchless Rome, the retreat of the solitary one during long months! – to civilized life – to the settled home and succession of monotonous days, farewell! Peril will now be mine; and I hail her as a friend – death will perpetually cross my path, and I will meet him as a benefactor; hardship, inclement weather, and dangerous tempests will be my sworn mates. Ye spirits of storm, receive me! ye powers of destruction, open wide your arms, and clasp me for ever! if a kinder power have not decreed another end, so that after long endurance I may reap my reward, and again feel my heart beat near the heart of another like to me.

Tiber, the road which is spread by nature's own hand, threading her continent, was at my feet, and many a boat was tethered to the banks. I would with a few books, provisions, and my dog, embark in one of these and float down the current of the stream into the sea; and then, keeping near land, I would coast the beauteous shores and sunny promontories of the blue Mediterranean, pass Naples, along Calabria, and would dare the twin perils of Scylla and Charybdis; then, with fearless aim, (for what had I to lose?) skim ocean's surface towards Malta and the further Cyclades. I would avoid Constantinople, the sight of whose well-known towers and inlets belonged to another state of existence from my present one; I would coast Asia Minor, and Syria, and, passing the seven-mouthed Nile, steer northward again, till losing sight of forgotten Carthage and deserted Lybia, I should reach the pillars of Hercules. And then – no matter where – the oozy caves, and soundless depths of ocean may be my dwelling, before I accomplish this long-drawn voyage, or the arrow of disease find my heart as I float singly on the weltering Mediterranean; or, in some place I touch at, I may find what I seek – a companion; or if this may not be – to endless time, decrepid and grey headed – youth already in the grave with those I love – the lone wanderer will still unfurl his sail, and clasp the tiller – and, still obeying the breezes of heaven, for ever round another and another promontory, anchoring in another and another bay, still ploughing seedless ocean, leaving behind the verdant land of native Europe, adown the tawny shore of Africa, having weathered the fierce seas of the Cape, I may moor my worn skiff in a creek, shaded by spicy groves of the odorous islands of the far Indian ocean.

These are wild dreams. Yet since, now a week ago, they came on me, as I stood on the height of St. Peter's, they have ruled my imagination.

I have chosen my boat, and laid in my scant stores. I have selected a few books; the principal are Homer and Shakespeare – But the libraries of the world are thrown open to me – and in any port I can renew my stock. I form no expectation of alteration for the better; but the monotonous present is intolerable to me. Neither hope nor joy are my pilots – restless despair and fierce desire of change lead me on. I long to grapple with danger, to be excited by fear, to have some task, however slight or voluntary, for each day's fulfilment. I shall witness all the variety of appearance, that the elements can assume – I shall read fair augury in the rainbow – menace in the cloud – some lesson or record dear to my heart in everything. Thus around the shores of deserted earth, while the sun is high, and the moon waxes or wanes, angels, the spirits of the dead, and the ever-open eye of the Supreme, will behold the tiny bark, freighted with Verney – the LAST MAN.

A Post-Apocalyptic Pandemic

Presented in its entirety, here is Jack London's *The Scarlet Plague,* which was first serialised in two instalments in the *London Magazine* and thereafter reprinted as a single volume by MacMillan publishers. It is an apocalyptic tale in which humanity has been decimated by a deadly disease known as the Red Death (the Black Death in all but name). London's novel was clearly inspired by two previous tales we have encountered in this book: Mary Shelley's *The Last Man* and Edgar Allan Poe's *Mask of the Red Death.* Yet the book also looks forward to modern-day pandemic-apocalypse movies and television shows.[26]

The Scarlet Plague by Jack London (1912)

I

The way led along upon what had once been the embankment of a railroad. But no train had run upon it for many years. The forest on either side swelled up the slopes of the embankment and crested across it in a green wave of trees and bushes. The trail was as narrow as a man's body, and was no more than a wild-animal runway. Occasionally, a piece of rusty iron, showing through the forest-mould, advertised that the rail and the ties still remained. In one place, a ten-inch tree, bursting through at a connection, had lifted the end of a rail clearly into view. The tie had evidently followed the rail, held to it by the spike long enough for its bed to be filled with gravel and rotten leaves, so that now the crumbling, rotten timber thrust itself up at a curious slant. Old as the road was, it was manifest that it had been of the mono-rail type.

An old man and a boy travelled along this runway. They moved slowly, for the old man was very old, a touch of palsy made his movements tremulous, and he leaned heavily upon his staff. A rude skull-cap of goat-skin protected his head from the sun. From beneath this fell a scant fringe of stained and dirty-white hair. A visor, ingeniously made from a large leaf, shielded his eyes, and from under this he peered at the way of his feet on the trail. His beard, which should have been snow-white but which showed the same weather-wear and camp-stain as his hair, fell nearly to his waist in a great tangled mass. About his chest and shoulders hung a single, mangy garment of goat-skin. His arms and legs, withered and skinny, betokened extreme age, as well as did their sunburn and scars and scratches betoken long years of exposure to the elements.

The boy, who led the way, checking the eagerness of his muscles to the slow progress of the elder, likewise wore a single garment – a ragged-edged piece of bear-skin, with a hole in the middle through which he had thrust his head. He could not have been more than twelve years old. Tucked coquettishly over one ear was the freshly severed tail of a pig. In one hand he carried a medium-sized bow and an arrow.

On his back was a quiverful of arrows. From a sheath hanging about his neck on a thong, projected the battered handle of a hunting knife. He was as brown as a berry, and walked softly, with almost a catlike tread. In marked contrast with his sunburned skin were his eyes – blue, deep blue, but keen and sharp as a pair of gimlets. They seemed to bore into all about him in a way that was habitual. As he went along he smelled things, as well, his distended, quivering nostrils carrying to his brain an endless series of messages from the outside world. Also, his hearing was acute, and had been so trained that it operated automatically. Without conscious effort, he heard all the slight sounds in the apparent quiet – heard, and differentiated, and classified these sounds – whether they were of the wind rustling the leaves, of the humming of bees and gnats, of the distant rumble of the sea that drifted to him only in lulls, or of the gopher, just under his foot, shoving a pouchful of earth into the entrance of his hole.

Suddenly he became alertly tense. Sound, sight, and odor had given him a simultaneous warning. His hand went back to the old man, touching him, and the pair stood still. Ahead, at one side of the top of the embankment, arose a crackling sound, and the boy's gaze was fixed on the tops of the agitated bushes. Then a large bear, a grizzly, crashed into view, and likewise stopped abruptly, at sight of the humans. He did not like them, and growled querulously. Slowly the boy fitted the arrow to the bow, and slowly he pulled the bowstring taut. But he never removed his eyes from the bear.

The old man peered from under his green leaf at the danger, and stood as quietly as the boy. For a few seconds this mutual scrutinizing went on; then, the bear betraying a growing irritability, the boy, with a movement of his head, indicated that the old man must step aside from the trail and go down the embankment. The boy followed, going backward, still holding the bow taut and ready. They waited till a crashing among the bushes from the opposite side of the embankment told them the bear had gone on. The boy grinned as he led back to the trail.

'A big un, Granser,' he chuckled.

The old man shook his head.

'They get thicker every day,' he complained in a thin, undependable falsetto. 'Who'd have thought I'd live to see the time when a man would be afraid of his life on the way to the Cliff House. When I was a boy, Edwin, men and women and little babies used to come out here from San Francisco by tens of thousands on a nice day. And there weren't any bears then. No, sir. They used to pay money to look at them in cages, they were that rare.'

'What is money, Granser?'

Before the old man could answer, the boy recollected and triumphantly shoved his hand into a pouch under his bear-skin and pulled forth a battered and tarnished silver dollar. The old man's eyes glistened, as he held the coin close to them.

'I can't see,' he muttered. 'You look and see if you can make out the date, Edwin.'

The boy laughed.

'You're a great Granser,' he cried delightedly, 'always making believe them little marks mean something.'

The old man manifested an accustomed chagrin as he brought the coin back again close to his own eyes.

'2012,' he shrilled, and then fell to cackling grotesquely. 'That was the year Morgan the Fifth was appointed President of the United States by the Board of Magnates. It must have been one of the last coins minted, for the Scarlet Death came in 2013. Lord! Lord! – think of it! Sixty years ago, and I am the only person alive to-day that lived in those times. Where did you find it, Edwin?'

The boy, who had been regarding him with the tolerant curiousness one accords to the prattlings of the feeble-minded, answered promptly.

'I got it off of Hoo-Hoo. He found it when we was herdin' goats down near San José last spring. Hoo-Hoo said it was *money*. Ain't you hungry, Granser?'

The ancient caught his staff in a tighter grip and urged along the trail, his old eyes shining greedily.

'I hope Hare-Lip's found a crab... or two,' he mumbled. 'They're good eating, crabs, mighty good eating when you've no more teeth and you've got grandsons that love their old grandsire and make a point of catching crabs for him. When I was a boy – '

But Edwin, suddenly stopped by what he saw, was drawing the bowstring on a fitted arrow. He had paused on the brink of a crevasse in the embankment. An ancient culvert had here washed out, and the stream, no longer confined, had cut a passage through the fill. On the opposite side, the end of a rail projected and overhung. It showed rustily through the creeping vines which overran it. Beyond, crouching by a bush, a rabbit looked across at him in trembling hesitancy. Fully fifty feet was the distance, but the arrow flashed true; and the transfixed rabbit, crying out in sudden fright and hurt, struggled painfully away into the brush. The boy himself was a flash of brown skin and flying fur as he bounded down the steep wall of the gap and up the other side. His lean muscles were springs of steel that released into graceful and efficient action. A hundred feet beyond, in a tangle of bushes, he overtook the wounded creature, knocked its head on a convenient tree-trunk, and turned it over to Granser to carry.

'Rabbit is good, very good,' the ancient quavered, 'but when it comes to a toothsome delicacy I prefer crab. When I was a boy – '

'Why do you say so much that ain't got no sense?' Edwin impatiently interrupted the other's threatened garrulousness.

The boy did not exactly utter these words, but something that remotely resembled them and that was more guttural and explosive and economical of qualifying phrases. His speech showed distant kinship with that of the old man, and the latter's speech was approximately an English that had gone through a bath of corrupt usage.

'What I want to know,' Edwin continued, 'is why you call crab "toothsome delicacy"? Crab is crab, ain't it? No one I never heard calls it such funny things.'

The old man sighed but did not answer, and they moved on in silence. The surf grew suddenly louder, as they emerged from the forest upon a stretch of sand dunes bordering the sea. A few goats were browsing among the sandy hillocks, and a skin-clad boy, aided by a wolfish-looking dog that was only faintly reminiscent of a collie, was watching them. Mingled with the roar of the surf was a continuous, deep-throated barking or bellowing, which came from a cluster of jagged rocks a hundred yards out from shore. Here huge sea-lions hauled themselves up to lie in the sun or battle with one another. In the immediate foreground arose the smoke of a fire, tended by a third savage-looking boy. Crouched near him were several wolfish dogs similar to the one that guarded the goats.

The old man accelerated his pace, sniffing eagerly as he neared the fire.

'Mussels!' he muttered ecstatically. 'Mussels! And ain't that a crab, Hoo-Hoo? Ain't that a crab? My, my, you boys are good to your old grandsire.'

Hoo-Hoo, who was apparently of the same age as Edwin, grinned. 'All you want, Granser. I got four.'

The old man's palsied eagerness was pitiful. Sitting down in the sand as quickly as his stiff limbs would let him, he poked a large rock-mussel from out of the coals. The heat had forced its shells apart, and the meat, salmon-colored, was thoroughly cooked. Between thumb and forefinger, in trembling haste, he caught the morsel and carried it to his mouth. But it was too hot, and the next moment was violently ejected. The old man spluttered with the pain, and tears ran out of his eyes and down his cheeks.

The boys were true savages, possessing only the cruel humor of the savage. To them the incident was excruciatingly funny, and they burst into loud laughter. Hoo-Hoo danced up and down, while Edwin rolled gleefully on the ground. The boy with the goats came running to join in the fun.

'Set 'em to cool, Edwin, set 'em to cool,' the old man besought, in the midst of his grief, making no attempt to wipe away the tears that still flowed from his eyes. 'And cool a crab, Edwin, too. You know your grandsire likes crabs.'

From the coals arose a great sizzling, which proceeded from the many mussels bursting open their shells and exuding their moisture. They were large shellfish, running from three to six inches in length. The boys raked them out with sticks and placed them on a large piece of driftwood to cool.

'When I was a boy, we did not laugh at our elders; we respected them.'

The boys took no notice, and Granser continued to babble an incoherent flow of complaint and censure. But this time he was more careful, and did not burn his mouth. All began to eat, using nothing but their hands and making loud mouth-noises and lip-smackings. The third boy, who was called Hare-Lip, slyly deposited a pinch of sand on a mussel the ancient was carrying to his mouth; and when the grit of it bit into the old fellow's mucous membrane and gums, the laughter was again uproarious. He was unaware that a joke had been played on him, and spluttered and spat until Edwin, relenting, gave him a gourd of fresh water with which to wash out his mouth.

'Where's them crabs, Hoo-Hoo?' Edwin demanded. 'Granser's set upon having a snack.'

Again Granser's eyes burned with greediness as a large crab was handed to him. It was a shell with legs and all complete, but the meat had long since departed. With shaky fingers and babblings of anticipation, the old man broke off a leg and found it filled with emptiness.

'The crabs, Hoo-Hoo?' he wailed. 'The crabs?'

'I was fooling Granser. They ain't no crabs! I never found one.'

The boys were overwhelmed with delight at sight of the tears of senile disappointment that dribbled down the old man's cheeks. Then, unnoticed, Hoo-Hoo replaced the empty shell with a fresh-cooked crab. Already dismembered, from the cracked legs the white meat sent forth a small cloud of savory steam. This attracted the old man's nostrils, and he looked down in amazement.

The change of his mood to one of joy was immediate. He snuffled and muttered and mumbled, making almost a croon of delight, as he began to eat. Of this the boys took little notice, for it was an accustomed spectacle. Nor did they notice his occasional exclamations and utterances of phrases which meant nothing to them, as, for instance, when he smacked his lips and champed his gums while muttering: 'Mayonnaise! Just think – mayonnaise! And it's sixty years since the last was ever made! Two generations and never a smell of it! Why, in those days it was served in every restaurant with crab.'

When he could eat no more, the old man sighed, wiped his hands on his naked legs, and gazed out over the sea. With the content of a full stomach, he waxed reminiscent.

'To think of it! I've seen this beach alive with men, women, and children on a pleasant Sunday. And there weren't any bears to eat them up, either. And right up there on the cliff was a big restaurant where you could get anything you wanted to eat. Four million people lived in San Francisco then. And now, in the whole city and county there aren't forty all told. And out there on the sea were ships and ships always to be seen, going in for the Golden Gate or coming out. And airships in the air – dirigibles and flying machines. They could travel two hundred miles an hour. The mail contracts with the New York and San Francisco Limited demanded that for the minimum. There was a chap, a Frenchman, I forget his name, who succeeded in making three hundred; but the thing was risky, too risky for conservative persons. But he was on the right clew, and he would have managed it if it hadn't been for the Great Plague. When I was a boy, there were men alive who remembered the coming of the first aeroplanes, and now I have lived to see the last of them, and that sixty years ago.'

The old man babbled on, unheeded by the boys, who were long accustomed to his garrulousness, and whose vocabularies, besides, lacked the greater portion of the words he used. It was noticeable that in these rambling soliloquies his English seemed to recrudesce into better construction and phraseology. But when he talked directly with the boys it lapsed, largely, into their own uncouth and simpler forms.

'But there weren't many crabs in those days,' the old man wandered on. 'They were fished out, and they were great delicacies. The open season was only a month long, too. And now crabs are accessible the whole year around. Think of it – catching all the crabs you want, any time you want, in the surf of the Cliff House beach!'

A sudden commotion among the goats brought the boys to their feet. The dogs about the fire rushed to join their snarling fellow who guarded the goats, while the goats themselves stampeded in the direction of their human protectors. A half dozen forms, lean and gray, glided about on the sand hillocks and faced the bristling dogs. Edwin arched an arrow that fell short. But Hare-Lip, with a sling such as David carried into battle against Goliath, hurled a stone through the air that whistled from the speed of its flight. It fell squarely among the wolves and caused them to slink away toward the dark depths of the eucalyptus forest.

The boys laughed and lay down again in the sand, while Granser sighed ponderously. He had eaten too much, and, with hands clasped on his paunch, the fingers interlaced, he resumed his maunderings.

'"The fleeting systems lapse like foam,"' he mumbled what was evidently a quotation. 'That's it – foam, and fleeting. All man's toil upon the planet was just so much foam. He domesticated the serviceable animals, destroyed the hostile ones, and cleared the land of its wild vegetation. And then he passed, and the flood of primordial life rolled back again, sweeping his handiwork away – the weeds and the forest inundated his fields, the beasts of prey swept over his flocks, and now there are wolves on the Cliff House beach.' He was appalled by the thought. 'Where four million people disported themselves, the wild wolves roam to-day, and the savage progeny of our loins, with prehistoric weapons, defend themselves against the fanged despoilers. Think of it! And all because of the Scarlet Death – '

The adjective had caught Hare-Lip's ear.

'He's always saying that,' he said to Edwin. 'What is *scarlet?*'

'"The scarlet of the maples can shake me like the cry of bugles going by,"' the old man quoted.

'It's red,' Edwin answered the question. 'And you don't know it because you come from the Chauffeur Tribe. They never did know nothing, none of them. Scarlet is red – I know that.'

'Red is red, ain't it?' Hare-Lip grumbled. 'Then what's the good of gettin' cocky and calling it scarlet?'

'Granser, what for do you always say so much what nobody knows?' he asked. 'Scarlet ain't anything, but red is red. Why don't you say red, then?'

'Red is not the right word,' was the reply. 'The plague was scarlet. The whole face and body turned scarlet in an hour's time. Don't I know? Didn't I see enough of it? And I am telling you it was scarlet because – well, because it *was* scarlet. There is no other word for it.'

'Red is good enough for me,' Hare-Lip muttered obstinately. 'My dad calls red red, and he ought to know. He says everybody died of the Red Death.'

'Your dad is a common fellow, descended from a common fellow,' Granser retorted heatedly. 'Don't I know the beginnings of the Chauffeurs? Your grandsire was a chauffeur, a servant, and without education. He worked for other persons. But your grandmother was of good stock, only the children did not take after her. Don't I remember when I first met them, catching fish at Lake Temescal?'

'What is *education?*' Edwin asked.

'Calling red scarlet,' Hare-Lip sneered, then returned to the attack on Granser. 'My dad told me, an' he got it from his dad afore he croaked, that your wife was a Santa Rosan, an' that she was sure no account. He said she was a *hash-slinger* before the Red Death, though I don't know what a *hash-slinger* is. You can tell me, Edwin.'

But Edwin shook his head in token of ignorance.

'It is true, she was a waitress,' Granser acknowledged. 'But she was a good woman, and your mother was her daughter. Women were very scarce in the days after the Plague. She was the only wife I could find, even if she was a *hash-slinger*, as your father calls it. But it is not nice to talk about our progenitors that way.'

'Dad says that the wife of the first Chauffeur was a *lady* – '

'What's a *lady*?' Hoo-Hoo demanded.

'A *lady*'s a Chauffeur squaw,' was the quick reply of Hare-Lip.

'The first Chauffeur was Bill, a common fellow, as I said before,' the old man expounded; 'but his wife was a lady, a great lady. Before the Scarlet Death she was the wife of Van Worden. He was President of the Board of Industrial Magnates, and was one of the dozen men who ruled America. He was worth one billion, eight hundred millions of dollars – coins like you have there in your pouch, Edwin. And then came the Scarlet Death, and his wife became the wife of Bill, the first Chauffeur. He used to beat her, too. I have seen it myself.'

Hoo-Hoo, lying on his stomach and idly digging his toes in the sand, cried out and investigated, first, his toe-nail, and next, the small hole he had dug. The other two boys joined him, excavating the sand rapidly with their hands till there lay three skeletons exposed. Two were of adults, the third being that of a part-grown child. The old man trudged along on the ground and peered at the find.

'Plague victims,' he announced. 'That's the way they died everywhere in the last days. This must have been a family, running away from the contagion and perishing here on the Cliff House beach. They – what are you doing, Edwin?'

This question was asked in sudden dismay, as Edwin, using the back of his hunting knife, began to knock out the teeth from the jaws of one of the skulls.

'Going to string 'em,' was the response.

The three boys were now hard at it; and quite a knocking and hammering arose, in which Granser babbled on unnoticed.

'You are true savages. Already has begun the custom of wearing human teeth. In another generation you will be perforating your noses and ears and wearing ornaments of bone and shell. I know. The human race is doomed to sink back farther and farther into the primitive night ere again it begins its bloody climb upward to civilization. When we increase and feel the lack of room, we will proceed to kill one another. And then I suppose you will wear human scalp-locks at your waist, as well – as you, Edwin, who are the gentlest of my grandsons, have already begun with that vile pigtail. Throw it away, Edwin, boy; throw it away.'

'What a gabble the old geezer makes,' Hare-Lip remarked, when, the teeth all extracted, they began an attempt at equal division.

They were very quick and abrupt in their actions, and their speech, in moments of hot discussion over the allotment of the choicer teeth, was truly a gabble. They spoke in monosyllables and short jerky sentences that was more a gibberish than a language. And yet, through it ran hints of grammatical construction, and appeared vestiges of the conjugation of some superior culture. Even the speech of Granser was so corrupt that were it put down literally it would be almost so much nonsense to the reader. This, however, was when he talked with the boys.

When he got into the full swing of babbling to himself, it slowly purged itself into pure English. The sentences grew longer and were enunciated with a rhythm and ease that was reminiscent of the lecture platform.

'Tell us about the Red Death, Granser,' Hare-Lip demanded, when the teeth affair had been satisfactorily concluded.

'The Scarlet Death,' Edwin corrected.

'An' don't work all that funny lingo on us,' Hare-Lip went on. 'Talk sensible, Granser, like a Santa Rosan ought to talk. Other Santa Rosans don't talk like you.'

II

The old man showed pleasure in being thus called upon. He cleared his throat and began.

'Twenty or thirty years ago my story was in great demand. But in these days nobody seems interested – '

'There you go!' Hare-Lip cried hotly. 'Cut out the funny stuff and talk sensible. What's *interested?* You talk like a baby that don't know how.'

'Let him alone,' Edwin urged, 'or he'll get mad and won't talk at all. Skip the funny places. We'll catch on to some of what he tells us.'

'Let her go, Granser,' Hoo-Hoo encouraged; for the old man was already maundering about the disrespect for elders and the reversion to cruelty of all humans that fell from high culture to primitive conditions.

The tale began.

'There were very many people in the world in those days. San Francisco alone held four millions – '

'What is millions?' Edwin interrupted.

Granser looked at him kindly.

'I know you cannot count beyond ten, so I will tell you. Hold up your two hands. On both of them you have altogether ten fingers and thumbs. Very well. I now take this grain of sand – you hold it, Hoo-Hoo.' He dropped the grain of sand into the lad's palm and went on. 'Now that grain of sand stands for the ten fingers of Edwin. I add another grain. That's ten more fingers. And I add another, and another, and another, until I have added as many grains as Edwin has fingers and thumbs. That makes what I call one hundred. Remember that word – one hundred. Now I put this pebble in Hare-Lip's hand. It stands for ten grains of sand, or ten tens of fingers, or one hundred fingers. I put in ten pebbles. They stand for a thousand fingers. I take a mussel-shell, and it stands for ten pebbles, or one hundred grains of sand, or one thousand fingers....' And so on, laboriously, and with much reiteration, he strove to build up in their minds a crude conception of numbers. As the quantities increased, he had the boys holding different magnitudes in each of their hands. For still higher sums, he laid the symbols on the log of driftwood; and for symbols he was hard put, being compelled to use the teeth from the skulls for millions, and the crab-shells for billions. It was here that he stopped, for the boys were showing signs of becoming tired.

'There were four million people in San Francisco – four teeth.'

The boys' eyes ranged along from the teeth and from hand to hand, down through the pebbles and sand-grains to Edwin's fingers. And back again they ranged along the ascending series in the effort to grasp such inconceivable numbers.

'That was a lot of folks, Granser,' Edwin at last hazarded.

'Like sand on the beach here, like sand on the beach, each grain of sand a man, or woman, or child. Yes, my boy, all those people lived right here in San Francisco. And at one time or another all those people came out on this very beach – more people than there are grains of sand. More – more – more. And San Francisco was a noble city. And across the bay – where we camped last year, even more people lived, clear from Point Richmond, on the level ground and on the hills, all the way around to San Leandro – one great city of seven million people. – Seven teeth... there, that's it, seven millions.'

Again the boys' eyes ranged up and down from Edwin's fingers to the teeth on the log.

'The world was full of people. The census of 2010 gave eight billions for the whole world – eight crab-shells, yes, eight billions. It was not like to-day. Mankind knew a great deal more about getting food. And the more food there was, the more people there were. In the year 1800, there were one hundred and seventy millions in Europe alone. One hundred years later – a grain of sand, Hoo-Hoo – one hundred years later, at 1900, there were five hundred millions in Europe – five grains of sand, Hoo-Hoo, and this one tooth. This shows how easy was the getting of food, and how men increased. And in the year 2000 there were fifteen hundred millions in Europe. And it was the same all over the rest of the world. Eight crab-shells there, yes, eight billion people were alive on the earth when the Scarlet Death began.

'I was a young man when the Plague came – twenty-seven years old; and I lived on the other side of San Francisco Bay, in Berkeley. You remember those great stone houses, Edwin, when we came down the hills from Contra Costa? That was where I lived, in those stone houses. I was a professor of English literature.'

Much of this was over the heads of the boys, but they strove to comprehend dimly this tale of the past.

'What was them stone houses for?' Hare-Lip queried.

'You remember when your dad taught you to swim?' The boy nodded. 'Well, in the University of California – that is the name we had for the houses – we taught young men and women how to think, just as I have taught you now, by sand and pebbles and shells, to know how many people lived in those days. There was very much to teach. The young men and women we taught were called students. We had large rooms in which we taught. I talked to them, forty or fifty at a time, just as I am talking to you now. I told them about the books other men had written before their time, and even, sometimes, in their time – '

'Was that all you did? – just talk, talk, talk?' Hoo-Hoo demanded. 'Who hunted your meat for you? and milked the goats? and caught the fish?'

'A sensible question, Hoo-Hoo, a sensible question. As I have told you, in those days food-getting was easy. We were very wise. A few men got the food for many men. The other men did other things. As you say, I talked. I talked all the time, and for this food was given me – much food, fine food, beautiful food, food that I have not tasted in sixty years and shall never taste again. I sometimes think the most wonderful achievement of our tremendous civilization was food – its inconceivable abundance, its infinite variety, its marvellous delicacy. O my grandsons, life was life in those days, when we had such wonderful things to eat.'

This was beyond the boys, and they let it slip by, words and thoughts, as a mere senile wandering in the narrative.

'Our food-getters were called *freemen*. This was a joke. We of the ruling classes owned all the land, all the machines, everything. These food-getters were our slaves. We took almost all the food they got, and left them a little so that they might eat, and work, and get us more food – '

'I'd have gone into the forest and got food for myself,' Hare-Lip announced; 'and if any man tried to take it away from me, I'd have killed him. '

The old man laughed.

'Did I not tell you that we of the ruling class owned all the land, all the forest, everything? Any food-getter who would not get food for us, him we punished or compelled to starve to death. And very few did that. They preferred to get food for us, and make clothes for us, and prepare and administer to us a thousand – a mussel-shell, Hoo-Hoo – a thousand satisfactions and delights. And I was Professor Smith in those days – Professor James Howard Smith. And my lecture courses were very popular – that is, very many of the young men and women liked to hear me talk about the books other men had written.

'And I was very happy, and I had beautiful things to eat. And my hands were soft, because I did no work with them, and my body was clean all over and dressed in the softest garments – ' He surveyed his mangy goat-skin with disgust.

'We did not wear such things in those days. Even the slaves had better garments. And we were most clean. We washed our faces and hands often every day. You boys never wash unless you fall into the water or go swimming.'

'Neither do you Granser,' Hoo-Hoo retorted.

'I know, I know, I am a filthy old man, but times have changed. Nobody washes these days, there are no conveniences. It is sixty years since I have seen a piece of soap. You do not know what soap is, and I shall not tell you, for I am telling the story of the Scarlet Death. You know what sickness is. We called it a disease. Very many of the diseases came from what we called germs. Remember that word – germs. A germ is a very small thing. It is like a woodtick, such as you find on the dogs in the spring of the year when they run in the forest. Only the germ is very small. It is so small that you cannot see it – '

Hoo-Hoo began to laugh.

'You're a queer un, Granser, talking about things you can't see. If you can't see 'em, how do you know they are? That's what I want to know. How do you know anything you can't see?'

'A good question, a very good question, Hoo-Hoo. But we did see – some of them. We had what we called microscopes and ultramicroscopes, and we put them to our eyes and looked through them, so that we saw things larger than they really were, and many things we could not see without the microscopes at all. Our best ultramicroscopes could make a germ look forty thousand times larger. A mussel-shell is a thousand fingers like Edwin's. Take forty mussel-shells, and by as many times larger was the germ when we looked at it through a microscope. And after that, we had other ways, by using what we called moving pictures, of making the forty-thousand-times germ many, many thousand times larger still. And thus we saw all these things which our eyes of themselves could not see. Take a grain of sand. Break it into ten pieces. Take one piece and break it into ten. Break one of those pieces into ten, and one of those into ten, and one of those into ten, and one of those into ten, and do it all day, and maybe, by sunset, you will have a piece as small as one of the germs.' The boys were openly incredulous. Hare-Lip sniffed and sneered and Hoo-Hoo snickered, until Edwin nudged them to be silent.

'The woodtick sucks the blood of the dog, but the germ, being so very small, goes right into the blood of the body, and there it has many children. In those days there would be as many as a billion – a crab-shell, please – as many as that crab-shell in one man's body. We called germs micro-organisms. When a few million, or a billion, of them were in a man, in all the blood of a man, he was sick. These germs were a disease. There were many different kinds of them – more different kinds than there are grains of sand on this beach. We knew only a few of the kinds. The micro-organic world was an invisible world, a world we could not see, and we knew very little about it. Yet we did know something. There was the *bacillus anthracis*; there was the *micrococcus*; there was the *Bacterium termo*, and the *Bacterium lactis* – that's what turns the goat milk sour even to this day, Hare-Lip; and there were *Schizomycetes* without end. And there were many others....'

Here the old man launched into a disquisition on germs and their natures, using words and phrases of such extraordinary length and meaninglessness, that the boys grinned at one another and looked out over the deserted ocean till they forgot the old man was babbling on.

'But the Scarlet Death, Granser,' Edwin at last suggested.

Granser recollected himself, and with a start tore himself away from the rostrum of the lecture-hall, where, to another world audience, he had been expounding the latest theory, sixty years gone, of germs and germ-diseases.

'Yes, yes, Edwin; I had forgotten. Sometimes the memory of the past is very strong upon me, and I forget that I am a dirty old man, clad in goat-skin, wandering with my savage grandsons who are goatherds in the primeval wilderness. "The fleeting systems lapse like foam", and so lapsed our glorious, colossal civilization. I am Granser, a tired old man. I belong to the tribe of Santa Rosans. I married into that tribe. My sons and daughters married into the Chauffeurs, the Sacramentos, and the Palo-Altos. You, Hare-Lip, are of the Chauffeurs. You, Edwin, are of the Sacramentos. And you, Hoo-Hoo, are of the Palo-Altos. Your tribe takes its name from a town that was near the seat of another great institution of learning. It was called Stanford University. Yes, I remember now. It is perfectly clear. I was telling you of the Scarlet Death. Where was I in my story?'

'You was telling about germs, the things you can't see but which make men sick,' Edwin prompted.

'Yes, that's where I was. A man did not notice at first when only a few of these germs got into his body. But each germ broke in half and became two germs, and they kept doing this very rapidly so that in a short time there were many millions of them in the body. Then the man was sick. He had a disease, and the disease was named after the kind of a germ that was in him. It might be measles, it might be influenza, it might be yellow fever; it might be any of thousands and thousands of kinds of diseases.

'Now this is the strange thing about these germs. There were always new ones coming to live in men's bodies. Long and long and long ago, when there were only a few men in the world, there were few diseases. But as men increased and lived closely together in great cities and civilizations, new diseases arose, new kinds of germs entered their bodies. Thus were countless millions and billions of human beings killed. And the more thickly men packed together, the more terrible were the new diseases that came to be. Long before my time, in the middle ages, there was the Black Plague that swept across Europe. It swept across Europe many times. There was tuberculosis, that entered into men wherever they were thickly packed. A hundred years before my time there was the bubonic plague. And in Africa was the sleeping sickness. The bacteriologists fought all these sicknesses and destroyed them, just as you boys fight the wolves away from your goats, or squash the mosquitoes that light on you. The bacteriologists – '

'But, Granser, what is a what-you-call-it?' Edwin interrupted.

'You, Edwin, are a goatherd. Your task is to watch the goats. You know a great deal about goats. A bacteriologist watches germs. That's his task, and he knows a great deal about them. So, as I was saying, the bacteriologists fought with the germs and destroyed them – sometimes. There was leprosy, a horrible disease. A hundred years before I was born, the bacteriologists discovered the germ of leprosy. They knew all about it. They made pictures of it. I have seen those pictures. But they never found a way to kill it. But in 1984, there was the Pantoblast Plague, a disease that broke out in a country called Brazil and that killed millions of people. But the bacteriologists found it out, and found the way to kill it, so that the Pantoblast Plague went no farther. They made what they called a serum, which they put into a man's body and which killed the pantoblast germs without killing the man. And in 1910, there was Pellagra, and also the hookworm. These were easily killed by the bacteriologists. But in 1947 there arose a new disease that had never been seen before. It got into the bodies of babies of only ten months old or less, and it made them unable to move their hands and feet, or to eat, or anything; and the bacteriologists were eleven years in discovering how to kill that particular germ and save the babies.

'In spite of all these diseases, and of all the new ones that continued to arise, there were more and more men in the world. This was because it was easy to get food. The easier it was to get food, the more men there were; the more men there were, the more thickly were they packed together on the earth; and the more thickly they were packed, the more new kinds of germs became diseases. There were warnings. Soldervetzsky, as early as 1929, told the bacteriologists that they had no guaranty against some new disease, a thousand times more deadly than any they knew, arising and killing by the hundreds of millions and even by the billion. You see, the micro-organic world remained a mystery to the end. They knew there was such a world, and that from time to time armies of new germs emerged from it to kill men.

'And that was all they knew about it. For all they knew, in that invisible micro-organic world there might be as many different kinds of germs as there are grains of sand on this beach. And also, in that same invisible world it might well be that new kinds of germs came to be. It might be there that life originated – the "abysmal fecundity," Soldervetzsky called it, applying the words of other men who had written before him....'

It was at this point that Hare-Lip rose to his feet, an expression of huge contempt on his face.

'Granser,' he announced, 'you make me sick with your gabble. Why don't you tell about the Red Death? If you ain't going to, say so, an' we'll start back for camp.'

The old man looked at him and silently began to cry. The weak tears of age rolled down his cheeks and all the feebleness of his eighty-seven years showed in his grief-stricken countenance.

'Sit down,' Edwin counselled soothingly. 'Granser's all right. He's just gettin' to the Scarlet Death, ain't you, Granser? He's just goin' to tell us about it right now. Sit down, Hare-Lip. Go ahead, Granser.'

III

The old man wiped the tears away on his grimy knuckles and took up the tale in a tremulous, piping voice that soon strengthened as he got the swing of the narrative.

'It was in the summer of 2013 that the Plague came. I was twenty-seven years old, and well do I remember it. Wireless despatches – '

Hare-Lip spat loudly his disgust, and Granser hastened to make amends.

'We talked through the air in those days, thousands and thousands of miles. And the word came of a strange disease that had broken out in New York. There were seventeen millions of people living then in that noblest city of America. Nobody thought anything about the news. It was only a small thing. There had been only a few deaths. It seemed, though, that they had died very quickly, and that one of the first signs of the disease was the turning red of the face and all the body. Within twenty-four hours came the report of the first case in Chicago. And on the same day, it was made public that London, the greatest city in the world, next to Chicago, had been secretly fighting the plague for two weeks and censoring the news despatches – that is, not permitting the word to go forth to the rest of the world that London had the plague.

'It looked serious, but we in California, like everywhere else, were not alarmed. We were sure that the bacteriologists would find a way to overcome this new germ, just as they had overcome other germs in the past. But the trouble was the astonishing quickness with which this germ destroyed human beings, and the fact that it inevitably killed any human body it entered. No one ever recovered. There was the old Asiatic cholera, when you might eat dinner with a well man in the evening, and the next morning, if you got up early enough, you would see him being hauled by your window in the death-cart. But this new plague was quicker than that – much quicker.

'From the moment of the first signs of it, a man would be dead in an hour. Some lasted for several hours. Many died within ten or fifteen minutes of the appearance of the first signs.

'The heart began to beat faster and the heat of the body to increase. Then came the scarlet rash, spreading like wildfire over the face and body. Most persons never noticed the increase in heat and heart-beat, and the first they knew was when the scarlet rash came out. Usually, they had convulsions at the time of the appearance of the rash. But these convulsions did not last long and were not very severe. If one lived through them, he became perfectly quiet, and only did he feel a numbness swiftly creeping up his body from the feet. The heels became numb first, then the legs, and hips, and when the numbness reached as high as his heart he died. They did not rave or sleep. Their minds always remained cool and calm up to the moment their heart numbed and stopped. And another strange thing was the rapidity of decomposition. No sooner was a person dead than the body seemed to fall to pieces, to fly apart, to melt away even as you looked at it. That was one of the reasons the plague spread so rapidly. All the billions of germs in a corpse were so immediately released.

'And it was because of all this that the bacteriologists had so little chance in fighting the germs. They were killed in their laboratories even as they studied the germ of the Scarlet Death. They were heroes. As fast as they perished, others stepped forth and took their places. It was in London that they first isolated it. The news was telegraphed everywhere. Trask was the name of the man who succeeded in this, but within thirty hours he was dead. Then came the struggle in all the laboratories to find something that would kill the plague germs. All drugs failed. You see, the problem was to get a drug, or serum, that would kill the germs in the body and not kill the body. They tried to fight it with other germs, to put into the body of a sick man germs that were the enemies of the plague germs – '

'And you can't see these germ-things, Granser,' Hare-Lip objected, 'and here you gabble, gabble, gabble about them as if they was anything, when they're nothing at all. Anything you can't see, ain't, that's what. Fighting things that ain't with things that ain't! They must have been all fools in them days. That's why they croaked. I ain't goin' to believe in such rot, I tell you that.'

Granser promptly began to weep, while Edwin hotly took up his defence.

'Look here, Hare-Lip, you believe in lots of things you can't see.'

Hare-Lip shook his head.

'You believe in dead men walking about. You never seen one dead man walk about.'

'I tell you I seen 'em, last winter, when I was wolf-hunting with dad.'

'Well, you always spit when you cross running water,' Edwin challenged.

'That's to keep off bad luck,' was Hare-Lip's defence.

'You believe in bad luck?'

'Sure.'

'An' you ain't never seen bad luck,' Edwin concluded triumphantly. 'You're just as bad as Granser and his germs. You believe in what you don't see. Go on, Granser.'

Hare-Lip, crushed by this metaphysical defeat, remained silent, and the old man went on. Often and often, though this narrative must not be clogged by the details, was Granser's tale interrupted while the boys squabbled among themselves. Also, among themselves they kept up a constant, low-voiced exchange of explanation and conjecture, as they strove to follow the old man into his unknown and vanished world.

'The Scarlet Death broke out in San Francisco. The first death came on a Monday morning. By Thursday they were dying like flies in Oakland and San Francisco. They died everywhere – in their beds, at their work, walking along the street. It was on Tuesday that I saw my first death – Miss Collbran, one of my students, sitting right there before my eyes, in my lecture-room. I noticed her face while I was talking. It had suddenly turned scarlet. I ceased speaking and could only look at her, for the first fear of the plague was already on all of us and we knew that it had come. The young women screamed and ran out of the room. So did the young men run out, all but two. Miss Collbran's convulsions were very mild and lasted less than a minute. One of the young men fetched her a glass of water. She drank only a little of it, and cried out: "My feet! All sensation has left them."

'After a minute she said, "I have no feet. I am unaware that I have any feet. And my knees are cold. I can scarcely feel that I have knees."

'She lay on the floor, a bundle of notebooks under her head. And we could do nothing. The coldness and the numbness crept up past her hips to her heart, and when it reached her heart she was dead. In fifteen minutes, by the clock – I timed it – she was dead, there, in my own classroom, dead. And she was a very beautiful, strong, healthy young woman. And from the first sign of the plague to her death only fifteen minutes elapsed. That will show you how swift was the Scarlet Death.

'Yet in those few minutes I remained with the dying woman in my classroom, the alarm had spread over the university; and the students, by thousands, all of them, had deserted the lecture-room and laboratories. When I emerged, on my way to make report to the President of the Faculty, I found the university deserted. Across the campus were several stragglers hurrying for their homes. Two of them were running.

'President Hoag, I found in his office, all alone, looking very old and very gray, with a multitude of wrinkles in his face that I had never seen before. At the sight of me, he pulled himself to his feet and tottered away to the inner office, banging the door after him and locking it. You see, he knew I had been exposed, and he was afraid. He shouted to me through the door to go away. I shall never forget my feelings as I walked down the silent corridors and out across that deserted campus. I was not afraid. I had been exposed, and I looked upon myself as already dead. It was not that, but a feeling of awful depression that impressed me. Everything had stopped. It was like the end of the world to me – my world. I had been born within sight and sound of the university. It had been my predestined career. My father had been a professor there before me, and his father before him. For a century and a half had this university, like a splendid machine, been running steadily on. And now, in an instant, it had stopped. It was like seeing the sacred flame die down on some thrice-sacred altar. I was shocked, unutterably shocked.

'When I arrived home, my housekeeper screamed as I entered, and fled away. And when I rang, I found the housemaid had likewise fled. I investigated. In the kitchen I found the cook on the point of departure. But she screamed, too, and in her haste dropped a suitcase of her personal belongings and ran out of the house and across the grounds, still screaming. I can hear her scream to this day. You see, we did not act in this way when ordinary diseases smote us. We were always calm over such things, and sent for the doctors and nurses who knew just what to do. But this was different. It struck so suddenly, and killed so swiftly, and never missed a stroke. When the scarlet rash appeared on a person's face, that person was marked by death. There was never a known case of a recovery.

'I was alone in my big house. As I have told you often before, in those days we could talk with one another over wires or through the air. The telephone bell rang, and I found my brother talking to me. He told me that he was not coming home for fear of catching the plague from me, and that he had taken our two sisters to stop at Professor Bacon's home. He advised me to remain where I was, and wait to find out whether or not I had caught the plague.

'To all of this I agreed, staying in my house and for the first time in my life attempting to cook. And the plague did not come out on me. By means of the telephone I could talk with whomsoever I pleased and get the news. Also, there were the newspapers, and I ordered all of them to be thrown up to my door so that I could know what was happening with the rest of the world.

'New York City and Chicago were in chaos. And what happened with them was happening in all the large cities. A third of the New York police were dead. Their chief was also dead, likewise the mayor. All law and order had ceased. The bodies were lying in the streets un-buried. All railroads and vessels carrying food and such things into the great city had ceased runnings and mobs of the hungry poor were pillaging the stores and warehouses. Murder and robbery and drunkenness were everywhere. Already the people had fled from the city by millions – at first the rich, in their private motor-cars and dirigibles, and then the great mass of the population, on foot, carrying the plague with them, themselves starving and pillaging the farmers and all the towns and villages on the way.

'The man who sent this news, the wireless operator, was alone with his instrument on the top of a lofty building. The people remaining in the city – he estimated them at several hundred thousand – had gone mad from fear and drink, and on all sides of him great fires were raging. He was a hero, that man who staid by his post – an obscure newspaperman, most likely.

'For twenty-four hours, he said, no transatlantic airships had arrived, and no more messages were coming from England. He did state, though, that a message from Berlin – that's in Germany – announced that Hoffmeyer, a bacteriologist of the Metchnikoff School, had discovered the serum for the plague. That was the last word, to this day, that we of America ever received from Europe. If Hoffmeyer discovered the serum, it was too late, or otherwise, long ere this, explorers from Europe would have come looking for us. We can only conclude that what happened in America happened in Europe, and that, at the best, some several score may have survived the Scarlet Death on that whole continent.

'For one day longer the despatches continued to come from New York. Then they, too, ceased. The man who had sent them, perched in his lofty building, had either died of the plague or been consumed in the great conflagrations he had described as raging around him. And what had occurred in New York had been duplicated in all the other cities. It was the same in San Francisco, and Oakland, and Berkeley. By Thursday the people were dying so rapidly that their corpses could not be handled, and dead bodies lay everywhere. Thursday night the panic outrush for the country began. Imagine, my grandsons, people, thicker than the salmon-run you have seen on the Sacramento river, pouring out of the cities by millions, madly over the country, in vain attempt to escape the ubiquitous death. You see, they carried the germs with them. Even the airships of the rich, fleeing for mountain and desert fastnesses, carried the germs.

'Hundreds of these airships escaped to Hawaii, and not only did they bring the plague with them, but they found the plague already there before them. This we learned, by the despatches, until all order in San Francisco vanished, and there were no operators left at their posts to receive or send. It was amazing, astounding, this loss of communication with the world. It was exactly as if the world had ceased, been blotted out. For sixty years that world has no longer existed for me. I know there must be such places as New York, Europe, Asia, and Africa; but not one word has been heard of them – not in sixty years. With the coming of the Scarlet Death the world fell apart, absolutely, irretrievably. Ten thousand years of culture and civilization passed in the twinkling of an eye, "lapsed like foam".

'I was telling about the airships of the rich. They carried the plague with them and no matter where they fled, they died. I never encountered but one survivor of any of them – Mungerson. He was afterwards a Santa Rosan, and he married my eldest daughter. He came into the tribe eight years after the plague. He was then nineteen years old, and he was compelled to wait twelve years more before he could marry. You see, there were no unmarried women, and some of the older daughters of the Santa Rosans were already bespoken. So he was forced to wait until my Mary had grown to sixteen years. It was his son, Gimp-Leg, who was killed last year by the mountain lion.

'Mungerson was eleven years old at the time of the plague. His father was one of the Industrial Magnates, a very wealthy, powerful man. It was on his airship, the Condor, that they were fleeing, with all the family, for the wilds of British Columbia, which is far to the north of here. But there was some accident, and they were wrecked near Mount Shasta. You have heard of that mountain. It is far to the north. The plague broke out amongst them, and this boy of eleven was the only survivor. For eight years he was alone, wandering over a deserted land and looking vainly for his own kind. And at last, travelling south, he picked up with us, the Santa Rosans.

'But I am ahead of my story. When the great exodus from the cities around San Francisco Bay began, and while the telephones were still working, I talked with my brother. I told him this flight from the cities was insanity, that there were no symptoms of the plague in me, and that the thing for us to do was to isolate ourselves and our relatives in some safe place. We decided on the Chemistry Building, at the university, and we planned to lay in a supply of provisions, and by force of arms to prevent any other persons from forcing their presence upon us after we had retired to our refuge.

'All this being arranged, my brother begged me to stay in my own house for at least twenty-four hours more, on the chance of the plague developing in me. To this I agreed, and he promised to come for me next day. We talked on over the details of the provisioning and the defending of the Chemistry Building until the telephone died. It died in the midst of our conversation. That evening there were no electric lights, and I was alone in my house in the darkness. No more newspapers were being printed, so I had no knowledge of what was taking place outside.

'I heard sounds of rioting and of pistol shots, and from my windows I could see the glare of the sky of some conflagration in the direction of Oakland. It was a night of terror. I did not sleep a wink. A man – why and how I do not know – was killed on the sidewalk in front of the house. I heard the rapid reports of an automatic pistol, and a few minutes later the wounded wretch crawled up to my door, moaning and crying out for help. Arming myself with two automatics, I went to him. By the light of a match I ascertained that while he was dying of the bullet wounds, at the same time the plague was on him. I fled indoors, whence I heard him moan and cry out for half an hour longer.

'In the morning, my brother came to me. I had gathered into a handbag what things of value I purposed taking, but when I saw his face I knew that he would never accompany me to the Chemistry

Building. The plague was on him. He intended shaking my hand, but I went back hurriedly before him.

'"Look at yourself in the mirror," I commanded.

'He did so, and at sight of his scarlet face, the color deepening as he looked at it, he sank down nervelessly in a chair.

'"My God!" he said. "I've got it. Don't come near me. I am a dead man."'

'Then the convulsions seized him. He was two hours in dying, and he was conscious to the last, complaining about the coldness and loss of sensation in his feet, his calves, his thighs, until at last it was his heart and he was dead.

'That was the way the Scarlet Death slew. I caught up my handbag and fled. The sights in the streets were terrible. One stumbled on bodies everywhere. Some were not yet dead. And even as you looked, you saw men sink down with the death fastened upon them. There were numerous fires burning in Berkeley, while Oakland and San Francisco were apparently being swept by vast conflagrations. The smoke of the burning filled the heavens, so that the midday was as a gloomy twilight, and, in the shifts of wind, sometimes the sun shone through dimly, a dull red orb. Truly, my grandsons, it was like the last days of the end of the world.

'There were numerous stalled motor cars, showing that the gasoline and the engine supplies of the garages had given out. I remember one such car. A man and a woman lay back dead in the seats, and on the pavement near it were two more women and a child. Strange and terrible sights there were on every hand. People slipped by silently, furtively, like ghosts – white-faced women carrying infants in their arms; fathers leading children by the hand; singly, and in couples, and in families – all fleeing out of the city of death. Some carried supplies of food, others blankets and valuables, and there were many who carried nothing.

'There was a grocery store – a place where food was sold. The man to whom it belonged – I knew him well – a quiet, sober, but stupid and obstinate fellow, was defending it. The windows and doors had been broken in, but he, inside, hiding behind a counter, was discharging his pistol at a number of men on the sidewalk who were breaking in. In the entrance were several bodies – of men, I decided, whom he had killed earlier in the day. Even as I looked on from a distance, I saw one of the robbers break the windows of the adjoining store, a place where shoes were sold, and deliberately set fire to it. I did not go to the groceryman's assistance. The time for such acts had already passed. Civilization was crumbling, and it was each for himself.'

IV

I went away hastily, down a cross-street, and at the first corner I saw another tragedy. Two men of the working class had caught a man and a woman with two children, and were robbing them. I knew the man by sight, though I had never been introduced to him. He was a poet whose verses I had long admired. Yet I did not go to his help, for at the moment I came upon the scene there was a pistol shot, and I saw him sinking to the ground. The woman screamed, and she was felled with a fist-blow by one of the brutes. I cried out threateningly, whereupon they discharged their pistols at me and I ran away around the corner. Here I was blocked by an advancing conflagration. The buildings on both sides were burning, and the street was filled with smoke and flame. From somewhere in that murk came a woman's voice calling shrilly for help. But I did not go to her. A man's heart turned to iron amid such scenes, and one heard all too many appeals for help.

'Returning to the corner, I found the two robbers were gone. The poet and his wife lay dead on the pavement. It was a shocking sight. The two children had vanished – whither I could not tell. And I knew, now, why it was that the fleeing persons I encountered slipped along so furtively and with such white faces. In the midst of our civilization, down in our slums and labor-ghettos, we had bred a race of barbarians, of savages; and now, in the time of our calamity, they turned upon us like the wild beasts they were and destroyed us. And they destroyed themselves as well.

'They inflamed themselves with strong drink and committed a thousand atrocities, quarreling and killing one another in the general madness. One group of workingmen I saw, of the better sort, who had banded together, and, with their women and children in their midst, the sick and aged in litters and being carried, and with a number of horses pulling a truck-load of provisions, they were fighting their way out of the city. They made a fine spectacle as they came down the street through the drifting smoke, though they nearly shot me when I first appeared in their path. As they went by, one of their leaders shouted out to me in apologetic explanation. He said they were killing the robbers and looters on sight, and that they had thus banded together as the only-means by which to escape the prowlers.

'It was here that I saw for the first time what I was soon to see so often. One of the marching men had suddenly shown the unmistakable mark of the plague. Immediately those about him drew away, and he, without a remonstrance, stepped out of his place to let them pass on. A woman, most probably his wife, attempted to follow him. She was leading a little boy by the hand. But the husband commanded her sternly to go on, while others laid hands on her and restrained her from following him. This I saw, and I saw the man also, with his scarlet blaze of face, step into a doorway on the opposite side of the street. I heard the report of his pistol, and saw him sink lifeless to the ground.

'After being turned aside twice again by advancing fires, I succeeded in getting through to the university. On the edge of the campus I came upon a party of university folk who were going in the direction of the Chemistry Building. They were all family men, and their families were with them, including the nurses and the servants. Professor Badminton greeted me, I had difficulty in recognizing him. Somewhere he had gone through flames, and his beard was singed off. About his head was a bloody bandage, and his clothes were filthy.

'He told me he had prowlers, and that his brother had been killed the previous night, in the defence of their dwelling.

'Midway across the campus, he pointed suddenly to Mrs. Swinton's face. The unmistakable scarlet was there. Immediately all the other women set up a screaming and began to run away from her. Her two children were with a nurse, and these also ran with the women. But her husband, Doctor Swinton, remained with her.

'"Go on, Smith," he told me. "Keep an eye on the children. As for me, I shall stay with my wife. I know she is as already dead, but I can't leave her. Afterwards, if I escape, I shall come to the Chemistry Building, and do you watch for me and let me in."'

'I left him bending over his wife and soothing her last moments, while I ran to overtake the party. We were the last to be admitted to the Chemistry Building. After that, with our automatic rifles we maintained our isolation. By our plans, we had arranged for a company of sixty to be in this refuge. Instead, every one of the number originally planned had added relatives and friends and whole families until there were over four hundred souls. But the Chemistry Building was large, and, standing by itself, was in no danger of being burned by the great fires that raged everywhere in the city.

'A large quantity of provisions had been gathered, and a food committee took charge of it, issuing rations daily to the various families and groups that arranged themselves into messes. A number of committees were appointed, and we developed a very efficient organization. I was on the committee of defence, though for the first day no prowlers came near. We could see them in the distance, however, and by the smoke of their fires knew that several camps of them were occupying the far edge of the campus. Drunkenness was rife, and often we heard them singing ribald songs or insanely shouting. While the world crashed to ruin about them and all the air was filled with the smoke of its burning, these low creatures gave rein to their bestiality and fought and drank and died. And after all, what did it matter? Everybody died anyway, the good and the bad, the efficients and the weaklings, those that loved to live and those that scorned to live. They passed. Everything passed.

'When twenty-four hours had gone by and no signs of the plague were apparent, we congratulated ourselves and set about digging a well. You have seen the great iron pipes which in those days carried water to all the city-dwellers. We feared that the fires in the city would burst the pipes and empty the reservoirs. So we tore up the cement floor of the central court of the Chemistry Building and dug a well. There were many young men, undergraduates, with us, and we worked night and day on the well. And our fears were confirmed. Three hours before we reached water, the pipes went dry.

'A second twenty-four hours passed, and still the plague did not appear among us. We thought we were saved. But we did not know what I afterwards decided to be true, namely, that the period of the incubation of the plague germs in a human's body was a matter of a number of days. It slew so swiftly when once it manifested itself, that we were led to believe that the period of incubation was equally swift. So, when two days had left us unscathed, we were elated with the idea that we were free of the contagion.

'But the third day disillusioned us. I can never forget the night preceding it. I had charge of the night guards from eight to twelve, and from the roof of the building I watched the passing of all man's glorious works. So terrible were the local conflagrations that all the sky was lighted up. One could read the finest print in the red glare. All the world seemed wrapped in flames. San Francisco spouted smoke and fire from a score of vast conflagrations that were like so many active volcanoes. Oakland, San Leandro, Haywards – all were burning; and to the northward, clear to Point Richmond, other fires were at work. It was an awe-inspiring spectacle. Civilization, my grandsons, civilization was passing in a sheet of flame and a breath of death. At ten o'clock that night, the great powder magazines at Point Pinole exploded in rapid succession. So terrific were the concussions that the strong building rocked as in an earthquake, while every pane of glass was broken. It was then that I left the roof and went down the long corridors, from room to room, quieting the alarmed women and telling them what had happened.

'An hour later, at a window on the ground floor, I heard pandemonium break out in the camps of the prowlers. There were cries and screams, and shots from many pistols. As we afterward conjectured, this fight had been precipitated by an attempt on the part of those that were well to drive out those that were sick. At any rate, a number of the plague-stricken prowlers escaped across the campus and drifted against our doors. We warned them back, but they cursed us and discharged a fusillade from their pistols. Professor Merryweather, at one of the windows, was instantly killed, the bullet striking him squarely between the eyes. We opened fire in turn, and all the prowlers fled away with the exception of three. One was a woman. The plague was on them and they were reckless. Like foul fiends, there in the red glare from the skies, with faces blazing, they continued to curse us and fire at us. One of the men I shot with my own hand. After that the other man and the woman, still cursing us, lay down under our windows, where we were compelled to watch them die of the plague.

'The situation was critical. The explosions of the powder magazines had broken all the windows of the Chemistry Building, so that we were exposed to the germs from the corpses. The sanitary committee was called upon to act, and it responded nobly. Two men were required to go out and remove the corpses, and this meant the probable sacrifice of their own lives, for, having performed the task, they were not to be permitted to re-enter the building. One of the professors, who was a bachelor, and one of the undergraduates volunteered. They bade good-bye to us and went forth. They were heroes. They gave up their lives that four hundred others might live. After they had performed their work, they stood for a moment, at a distance, looking at us wistfully. Then they waved their hands in farewell and went away slowly across the campus toward the burning city.

'And yet it was all useless. The next morning the first one of us was smitten with the plague – a little nurse-girl in the family of Professor Stout. It was no time for weak-kneed, sentimental policies. On the chance that she might be the only one, we thrust her forth from the building and commanded her to be gone.

'She went away slowly across the campus, wringing her hands and crying pitifully. We felt like brutes, but what were we to do? There were four hundred of us, and individuals had to be sacrificed.

'In one of the laboratories three families had domiciled themselves, and that afternoon we found among them no less than four corpses and seven cases of the plague in all its different stages.

'Then it was that the horror began. Leaving the dead lie, we forced the living ones to segregate themselves in another room. The plague began to break out among the rest of us, and as fast as the symptoms appeared, we sent the stricken ones to these segregated rooms. We compelled them to walk there by themselves, so as to avoid laying hands on them. It was heartrending. But still the plague raged among us, and room after room was filled with the dead and dying. And so we who were yet clean retreated to the next floor and to the next, before this sea of the dead, that, room by room and floor by floor, inundated the building.

'The place became a charnel house, and in the middle of the night the survivors fled forth, taking nothing with them except arms and ammunition and a heavy store of tinned foods. We camped on the opposite side of the campus from the prowlers, and, while some stood guard, others of us volunteered to scout into the city in quest of horses, motor cars, carts, and wagons, or anything that would carry our provisions and enable us to emulate the banded workingmen I had seen fighting their way out to the open country.

'I was one of these scouts; and Doctor Hoyle, remembering that his motor car had been left behind in his home garage, told me to look for it. We scouted in pairs, and Dombey, a young undergraduate, accompanied me. We had to cross half a mile of the residence portion of the city to get to Doctor Hoyle's home. Here the buildings stood apart, in the midst of trees and grassy lawns, and here the fires had played freaks, burning whole blocks, skipping blocks and often skipping a single house in a block. And here, too, the prowlers were still at their work. We carried our automatic pistols openly in our hands, and looked desperate enough, forsooth, to keep them from attacking us. But at Doctor Hoyle's house the thing happened. Untouched by fire, even as we came to it the smoke of flames burst forth.

'The miscreant who had set fire to it staggered down the steps and out along the driveway. Sticking out of his coat pockets were bottles of whiskey, and he was very drunk. My first impulse was to shoot him, and I have never ceased regretting that I did not. Staggering and maundering to himself, with bloodshot eyes, and a raw and bleeding slash down one side of his bewhiskered face, he was altogether the most nauseating specimen of degradation and filth I had ever encountered. I did not shoot him, and he leaned against a tree on the lawn to let us go by. It was the most absolute, wanton act. Just as we were opposite him, he suddenly drew a pistol and shot Dombey through the head. The next instant I shot him. But it was too late. Dombey expired without a groan, immediately. I doubt if he even knew what had happened to him.

'Leaving the two corpses, I hurried on past the burning house to the garage, and there found Doctor Hoyle's motor car. The tanks were filled with gasoline, and it was ready for use. And it was in this car that I threaded the streets of the ruined city and came back to the survivors on the campus. The other scouts returned, but none had been so fortunate. Professor Fairmead had found a Shetland pony, but the poor creature, tied in a stable and abandoned for days, was so weak from want of food and water that it could carry no burden at all. Some of the men were for turning it loose, but I insisted that we should lead it along with us, so that, if we got out of food, we would have it to eat.

'There were forty-seven of us when we started, many being women and children. The President of the Faculty, an old man to begin with, and now hopelessly broken by the awful happenings of the past week, rode in the motor car with several young children and the aged mother of Professor Fairmead. Wathope, a young professor of English, who had a grievous bullet-wound in his leg, drove the car. The rest of us walked, Professor Fairmead leading the pony.

'It was what should have been a bright summer day, but the smoke from the burning world filled the sky, through which the sun shone murkily, a dull and lifeless orb, blood-red and ominous. But we had grown accustomed to that blood-red sun. With the smoke it was different. It bit into our nostrils and eyes, and there was not one of us whose eyes were not bloodshot. We directed our course to the southeast through the endless miles of suburban residences, travelling along where the first swells of low hills rose from the flat of the central city. It was by this way, only, that we could expect to gain the country.

'Our progress was painfully slow. The women and children could not walk fast. They did not dream of walking, my grandsons, in the way all people walk to-day. In truth, none of us knew how to walk. It was not until after the plague that I learned really to walk. So it was that the pace of the slowest was the pace of all, for we dared not separate on account of the prowlers. There were not so many now of these human beasts of prey. The plague had already well diminished their numbers, but enough still lived to be a constant menace to us. Many of the beautiful residences were untouched by fire, yet smoking ruins were everywhere. The prowlers, too, seemed to have got over their insensate desire to burn, and it was more rarely that we saw houses freshly on fire.

'Several of us scouted among the private garages in search of motor cars and gasoline. But in this we were unsuccessful. The first great flights from the cities had swept all such utilities away. Calgan, a fine young man, was lost in this work. He was shot by prowlers while crossing a lawn. Yet this was our only casualty, though, once, a drunken brute deliberately opened fire on all of us. Luckily, he fired wildly, and we shot him before he had done any hurt.

'At Fruitvale, still in the heart of the magnificent residence section of the city, the plague again smote us. Professor Fairmead was the victim. Making signs to us that his mother was not to know, he turned aside into the grounds of a beautiful mansion. He sat down forlornly on the steps of the front veranda, and I, having lingered, waved him a last farewell. That night, several miles beyond Fruitvale and still in the city, we made camp. And that night we shifted camp twice to get away from our dead. In the morning there were thirty of us. I shall never forget the President of the Faculty. During the morning's march his wife, who was walking, betrayed the fatal symptoms, and when she drew aside to let us go on, he insisted on leaving the motor car and remaining with her. There was quite a discussion about this, but in the end we gave in. It was just as well, for we knew not which ones of us, if any, might ultimately escape.

'That night, the second of our march, we camped beyond Haywards in the first stretches of country. And in the morning there were eleven of us that lived. Also, during the night, Wathope, the professor with the wounded leg, deserted us in the motor car. He took with him his sister and his mother and most of our tinned provisions. It was that day, in the afternoon, while resting by the wayside, that I saw the last airship I shall ever see. The smoke was much thinner here in the country, and I first sighted the ship drifting and veering helplessly at an elevation of two thousand feet. What had happened I could not conjecture, but even as we looked we saw her bow dip down lower and lower. Then the bulkheads of the various gas-chambers must have burst, for, quite perpendicular, she fell like a plummet to the earth.

'And from that day to this I have not seen another airship. Often and often, during the next few years, I scanned the sky for them, hoping against hope that somewhere in the world civilization had survived. But it was not to be. What happened with us in California must have happened with everybody everywhere.

'Another day, and at Niles there were three of us. Beyond Niles, in the middle of the highway, we found Wathope. The motor car had broken down, and there, on the rugs which they had spread on the ground, lay the bodies of his sister, his mother, and himself.

'Wearied by the unusual exercise of continual walking, that night I slept heavily. In the morning I was alone in the world. Canfield and Parsons, my last companions, were dead of the plague. Of the four hundred that sought shelter in the Chemistry Building, and of the forty-seven that began the march, I alone remained – I and the Shetland pony. Why this should be so there is no explaining. I did not catch the plague, that is all. I was immune. I was merely the one lucky man in a million – just as every survivor was one in a million, or, rather, in several millions, for the proportion was at least that.'

V

'For two days I sheltered in a pleasant grove where there had been no deaths. In those two days, while badly depressed and believing that my turn would come at any moment, nevertheless I rested and recuperated. So did the pony. And on the third day, putting what small store of tinned provisions I possessed on the pony's back, I started on across a very lonely land. Not a live man, woman, or child, did I encounter, though the dead were everywhere. Food, however, was abundant. The land then was not as it is now. It was all cleared of trees and brush, and it was cultivated. The food for millions of mouths was growing, ripening, and going to waste. From the fields and orchards I gathered vegetables, fruits, and berries. Around the deserted farmhouses I got eggs and caught chickens. And frequently I found supplies of tinned provisions in the store-rooms.

'A strange thing was what was taking place with all the domestic animals. Everywhere they were going wild and preying on one another. The chickens and ducks were the first to be destroyed, while the pigs were the first to go wild, followed by the cats. Nor were the dogs long in adapting themselves to the changed conditions. There was a veritable plague of dogs. They devoured the corpses, barked and howled during the nights, and in the daytime slunk about in the distance. As the time went by, I noticed a change in their behavior. At first they were apart from one another, very suspicious and very prone to fight. But after a not very long while they began to come together and run in packs. The dog, you see, always was a social animal, and this was true before ever he came to be domesticated by man. In the last days of the world before the plague, there were many many very different kinds of dogs – dogs without hair and dogs with warm fur, dogs so small that they would make scarcely a mouthful for other dogs that were as large as mountain lions. Well, all the small dogs, and the weak types, were killed by their fellows. Also, the very large ones were not adapted for the wild life and bred out. As a result, the many different kinds of dogs disappeared, and there remained, running in packs, the medium-sized wolfish dogs that you know to-day.'

'But the cats don't run in packs, Granser,' Hoo-Hoo objected.

'The cat was never a social animal. As one writer in the nineteenth century said, the cat walks by himself. He always walked by himself, from before the time he was tamed by man, down through the long ages of domestication, to to-day when once more he is wild.

'The horses also went wild, and all the fine breeds we had degenerated into the small mustang horse you know to-day. The cows likewise went wild, as did the pigeons and the sheep. And that a few of the chickens survived you know yourself. But the wild chicken of to-day is quite a different thing from the chickens we had in those days.

'But I must go on with my story. I travelled through a deserted land. As the time went by I began to yearn more and more for human beings. But I never found one, and I grew lonelier and lonelier. I crossed Livermore Valley and the mountains between it and the great valley of the San Joaquin. You have never seen that valley, but it is very large and it is the home of the wild horse. There are great droves there, thousands and tens of thousands. I revisited it thirty years after, so I know. You think there are lots of wild horses down here in the coast valleys, but they are as nothing compared with those of the San Joaquin. Strange to say, the cows, when they went wild, went back into the lower mountains. Evidently they were better able to protect themselves there.

'In the country districts the ghouls and prowlers had been less in evidence, for I found many villages and towns untouched by fire. But they were filled by the pestilential dead, and I passed by without exploring them. It was near Lathrop that, out of my loneliness, I picked up a pair of collie dogs that were so newly free that they were urgently willing to return to their allegiance to man. These collies accompanied me for many years, and the strains of them are in those very dogs there that you boys have to-day. But in sixty years the collie strain has worked out. These brutes are more like domesticated wolves than anything else.'

Hare-Lip rose to his feet, glanced to see that the goats were safe, and looked at the sun's position in the afternoon sky, advertising impatience at the prolixity of the old man's tale. Urged to hurry by Edwin, Granser went on.

'There is little more to tell. With my two dogs and my pony, and riding a horse I had managed to capture, I crossed the San Joaquin and went on to a wonderful valley in the Sierras called Yosemite. In the great hotel there I found a prodigious supply of tinned provisions. The pasture was abundant, as was the game, and the river that ran through the valley was full of trout. I remained there three years in an utter loneliness that none but a man who has once been highly civilized can understand. Then I could stand it no more. I felt that I was going crazy. Like the dog, I was a social animal and I needed my kind. I reasoned that since I had survived the plague, there was a possibility that others had survived. Also, I reasoned that after three years the plague germs must all be gone and the land be clean again.

'With my horse and dogs and pony, I set out. Again I crossed the San Joaquin Valley, the mountains beyond, and came down into Livermore

Valley. The change in those three years was amazing. All the land had been splendidly tilled, and now I could scarcely recognize it, such was the sea of rank vegetation that had overrun the agricultural handiwork of man. You see, the wheat, the vegetables, and orchard trees had always been cared for and nursed by man, so that they were soft and tender. The weeds and wild bushes and such things, on the contrary, had always been fought by man, so that they were tough and resistant. As a result, when the hand of man was removed, the wild vegetation smothered and destroyed practically all the domesticated vegetation. The coyotes were greatly increased, and it was at this time that I first encountered wolves, straying in twos and threes and small packs down from the regions where they had always persisted.

'It was at Lake Temescal, not far from the one-time city of Oakland, that I came upon the first live human beings. Oh, my grandsons, how can I describe to you my emotion, when, astride my horse and dropping down the hillside to the lake, I saw the smoke of a campfire rising through the trees. Almost did my heart stop beating. I felt that I was going crazy. Then I heard the cry of a babe – a human babe. And dogs barked, and my dogs answered. I did not know but what I was the one human alive in the whole world. It could not be true that here were others – smoke, and the cry of a babe.

'Emerging on the lake, there, before my eyes, not a hundred yards away, I saw a man, a large man. He was standing on an outjutting rock and fishing. I was overcome. I stopped my horse. I tried to call out but could not. I waved my hand. It seemed to me that the man looked at me, but he did not appear to wave. Then I laid my head on my arms there in the saddle. I was afraid to look again, for I knew it was an hallucination, and I knew that if I looked the man would be gone. And so precious was the hallucination, that I wanted it to persist yet a little while. I knew, too, that as long as I did not look it would persist.

'Thus I remained, until I heard my dogs snarling, and a man's voice. What do you think the voice said? I will tell you. It said: "*Where in hell did you come from?*"'

'Those were the words, the exact words. That was what your other grandfather said to me, Hare-Lip, when he greeted me there on the shore of Lake Temescal fifty-seven years ago. And they were the most ineffable words I have ever heard. I opened my eyes, and there he stood before me, a large, dark, hairy man, heavy-jawed, slant-browed, fierce-eyed. How I got off my horse I do not know. But it seemed that the next I knew I was clasping his hand with both of mine and crying. I would have embraced him, but he was ever a narrow-minded, suspicious man, and he drew away from me. Yet did I cling to his hand and cry.'

Granser's voice faltered and broke at the recollection, and the weak tears streamed down his cheeks while the boys looked on and giggled.

'Yet did I cry,' he continued, 'and desire to embrace him, though the Chauffeur was a brute, a perfect brute – the most abhorrent man I have ever known. His name was... strange, how I have forgotten his name. Everybody called him Chauffeur – it was the name of his occupation, and it stuck. That is how, to this day, the tribe he founded is called the Chauffeur Tribe.

'He was a violent, unjust man. Why the plague germs spared him I can never understand. It would seem, in spite of our old metaphysical notions about absolute justice, that there is no justice in the universe. Why did he live? – an iniquitous, moral monster, a blot on the face of nature, a cruel, relentless, bestial cheat as well. All he could talk about was motor cars, machinery, gasoline, and garages – and especially, and with huge delight, of his mean pilferings and sordid swindlings of the persons who had employed him in the days before the coming of the plague. And yet he was spared, while hundreds of millions, yea, billions, of better men were destroyed.

'I went on with him to his camp, and there I saw her, Vesta, the one woman. It was glorious and... pitiful. There she was, Vesta Van Warden, the young wife of John Van Warden, clad in rags, with marred and scarred and toil-calloused hands, bending over the campfire and doing scullion work – she, Vesta, who had been born to the purple of the greatest baronage of wealth the world had ever known. John Van Warden, her husband, worth one billion, eight hundred millions and President of the Board of Industrial Magnates, had been the ruler of America. Also, sitting on the International Board of Control, he had been one of the seven men who ruled the world. And she herself had come of equally noble stock. Her father, Philip Saxon, had been President of the Board of Industrial Magnates up to the time of his death. This office was in process of becoming hereditary, and had Philip Saxon had a son that son would have succeeded him. But his only child was Vesta, the perfect flower of generations of the highest culture this planet has ever produced. It was not until the engagement between Vesta and Van Warden took place, that Saxon indicated the latter as his successor. It was, I am sure, a political marriage. I have reason to believe that Vesta never really loved her husband in the mad passionate way of which the poets used to sing. It was more like the marriages that obtained among crowned heads in the days before they were displaced by the Magnates.

'And there she was, boiling fish-chowder in a soot-covered pot, her glorious eyes inflamed by the acrid smoke of the open fire. Hers was a sad story. She was the one survivor in a million, as I had been, as the Chauffeur had been. On a crowning eminence of the Alameda Hills, overlooking San Francisco Bay, Van Warden had built a vast summer palace. It was surrounded by a park of a thousand acres. When the plague broke out, Van Warden sent her there. Armed guards patrolled the boundaries of the park, and nothing entered in the way of provisions or even mail matter that was not first fumigated. And yet did the plague enter, killing the guards at their posts, the servants at their tasks, sweeping away the whole army of retainers – or, at least, all of them who did not flee to die elsewhere. So it was that Vesta found herself the sole living person in the palace that had become a charnel house.

'Now the Chauffeur had been one of the servants that ran away. Returning, two months afterward, he discovered Vesta in a little summer pavilion where there had been no deaths and where she had established herself. He was a brute. She was afraid, and she ran away and hid among the trees. That night, on foot, she fled into the mountains – she, whose tender feet and delicate body had never known the bruise of stones nor the scratch of briars. He followed, and that night he caught her. He struck her. Do you understand? He beat her with those terrible fists of his and made her his slave. It was she who had to gather the firewood, build the fires, cook, and do all the degrading camp-labor – she, who had never performed a menial act in her life. These things he compelled her to do, while he, a proper savage, elected to lie around camp and look on. He did nothing, absolutely nothing, except on occasion to hunt meat or catch fish.'

'Good for Chauffeur,' Hare-Lip commented in an undertone to the other boys. 'I remember him before he died. He was a corker. But he did things, and he made things go. You know, Dad married his daughter, an' you ought to see the way he knocked the spots outa Dad. The Chauffeur was a son-of-a-gun. He made us kids stand around. Even when he was croaking he reached out for me, once, an' laid my head open with that long stick he kept always beside him.'

Hare-Lip rubbed his bullet head reminiscently, and the boys returned to the old man, who was maundering ecstatically about Vesta, the squaw of the founder of the Chauffeur Tribe.

'And so I say to you that you cannot understand the awfulness of the situation. The Chauffeur was a servant, understand, a servant. And he cringed, with bowed head, to such as she. She was a lord of life, both by birth and by marriage. The destinies of millions, such as he, she carried in the hollow of her pink-white hand. And, in the days before the plague, the slightest contact with such as he would have been pollution. Oh, I have seen it. Once, I remember, there was Mrs. Goldwin, wife of one of the great magnates. It was on a landing stage, just as she was embarking in her private dirigible, that she dropped her parasol. A servant picked it up and made the mistake of handing it to her – to her, one of the greatest royal ladies of the land! She shrank back, as though he were a leper, and indicated her secretary to receive it. Also, she ordered her secretary to ascertain the creature's name and to see that he was immediately discharged from service. And such a woman was Vesta Van Warden. And her the Chauffeur beat and made his slave.

' – Bill – that was it; Bill, the Chauffeur. That was his name. He was a wretched, primitive man, wholly devoid of the finer instincts and chivalrous promptings of a cultured soul. No, there is no absolute justice, for to him fell that wonder of womanhood, Vesta Van Warden. The grievousness of this you will never understand, my grandsons; for you are yourselves primitive little savages, unaware of aught else but savagery. Why should Vesta not have been mine? I was a man of culture and refinement, a professor in a great university. Even so, in the time before the plague, such was her exalted position, she would not have deigned to know that I existed. Mark, then, the abysmal degradation to which she fell at the hands of the Chauffeur. Nothing less than the destruction of all mankind had made it possible that I should know her, look in her eyes, converse with her, touch her hand – ay, and love her and know that her feelings toward me were very kindly. I have reason to believe that she, even she, would have loved me, there being no other man in the world except the Chauffeur. Why, when it destroyed eight billions of souls, did not the plague destroy just one more man, and that man the Chauffeur?

'Once, when the Chauffeur was away fishing, she begged me to kill him. With tears in her eyes she begged me to kill him. But he was a strong and violent man, and I was afraid. Afterwards, I talked with him. I offered him my horse, my pony, my dogs, all that I possessed, if he would give Vesta to me. And he grinned in my face and shook his head. He was very insulting. He said that in the old days he had been a servant, had been dirt under the feet of men like me and of women like Vesta, and that now he had the greatest lady in the land to be servant to him and cook his food and nurse his brats. "You had your day before the plague," he said; "but this is my day, and a damned good day it is. I wouldn't trade back to the old times for anything." Such words he spoke, but they are not his words. He was a vulgar, low-minded man, and vile oaths fell continually from his lips.

'Also, he told me that if he caught me making eyes at his woman he'd wring my neck and give her a beating as well. What was I to do? I was afraid. He was a brute. That first night, when I discovered the camp, Vesta and I had great talk about the things of our vanished world. We talked of art, and books, and poetry; and the Chauffeur listened and grinned and sneered. He was bored and angered by our way of speech which he did not comprehend, and finally he spoke up and said: "And this is Vesta Van Warden, one-time wife of Van Warden the Magnate – a high and stuck-up beauty, who is now my squaw. Eh, Professor Smith, times is changed, times is changed. Here, you, woman, take off my moccasins, and lively about it. I want Professor Smith to see how well I have you trained."'

'I saw her clench her teeth, and the flame of revolt rise in her face. He drew back his gnarled fist to strike, and I was afraid, and sick at heart. I could do nothing to prevail against him. So I got up to go, and not be witness to such indignity. But the Chauffeur laughed and threatened me with a beating if I did not stay and behold. And I sat there, perforce, by the campfire on the shore of Lake Temescal, and saw Vesta, Vesta Van Warden, kneel and remove the moccasins of that grinning, hairy, apelike human brute.

' – Oh, you do not understand, my grandsons. You have never known anything else, and you do not understand.

'"Halter-broke and bridle-wise," the Chauffeur gloated, while she performed that dreadful, menial task. "A trifle balky at times, Professor, a trifle balky; but a clout alongside the jaw makes her as meek and gentle as a lamb."'

'And another time he said: "We've got to start all over and replenish the earth and multiply. You're handicapped, Professor. You ain't got no wife, and we're up against a regular Garden-of-Eden proposition. But I ain't proud. I'll tell you what, Professor." He pointed at their little infant, barely a year old. "There's your wife, though you'll have to wait till she grows up. It's rich, ain't it? We're all equals here, and I'm the biggest toad in the splash. But I ain't stuck up – not I. I do you the honor, Professor Smith, the very great honor of betrothing to you my and Vesta Van Warden's daughter. Ain't it cussed bad that Van Warden ain't here to see?"'

VI

'I lived three weeks of infinite torment there in the Chauffeur's camp. And then, one day, tiring of me, or of what to him was my bad effect on Vesta, he told me that the year before, wandering through the Contra Costa Hills to the Straits of Carquinez, across the Straits he had seen a smoke. This meant that there were still other human beings, and that for three weeks he had kept this inestimably precious information from me. I departed at once, with my dogs and horses, and journeyed across the Contra Costa Hills to the Straits. I saw no smoke on the other side, but at Port Costa discovered a small steel barge on which I was able to embark my animals. Old canvas which I found served me for a sail, and a southerly breeze fanned me across the Straits and up to the ruins of Vallejo. Here, on the outskirts of the city, I found evidences of a recently occupied camp.

'Many clam-shells showed me why these humans had come to the shores of the Bay. This was the Santa Rosa Tribe, and I followed its track along the old railroad right of way across the salt marshes to Sonoma Valley. Here, at the old brickyard at Glen Ellen, I came upon the camp. There were eighteen souls all told. Two were old men, one of whom was Jones, a banker. The other was Harrison, a retired pawnbroker, who had taken for wife the matron of the State Hospital for the Insane at Napa. Of all the persons of the city of Napa, and of all the other towns and villages in that rich and populous valley, she had been the only survivor. Next, there were the three young men – Cardiff and Hale, who had been farmers, and Wainwright, a common day-laborer. All three had found wives. To Hale, a crude, illiterate farmer, had fallen Isadore, the greatest prize, next to Vesta, of the women who came through the plague. She was one of the world's most noted singers, and the plague had caught her at San Francisco. She has talked with me for hours at a time, telling me of her adventures, until, at last, rescued by Hale in the Mendocino Forest Reserve, there had remained nothing for her to do but become his wife. But Hale was a good fellow, in spite of his illiteracy. He had a keen sense of justice and right-dealing, and she was far happier with him than was Vesta with the Chauffeur.

'The wives of Cardiff and Wainwright were ordinary women, accustomed to toil with strong constitutions – just the type for the wild new life which they were compelled to live. In addition were two adult idiots from the feeble-minded home at Eldredge, and five or six young children and infants born after the formation of the Santa Rosa Tribe. Also, there was Bertha. She was a good woman, Hare-Lip, in spite of the sneers of your father. Her I took for wife. She was the mother of your father, Edwin, and of yours, Hoo-Hoo. And it was our daughter, Vera, who married your father, Hare-Lip – your father, Sandow, who was the oldest son of Vesta Van Warden and the Chauffeur.

'And so it was that I became the nineteenth member of the Santa Rosa Tribe. There were only two outsiders added after me. One was Mungerson, descended from the Magnates, who wandered alone in the wilds of Northern California for eight years before he came south and joined us. He it was who waited twelve years more before he married my daughter, Mary. The other was Johnson, the man who founded the Utah Tribe. That was where he came from, Utah, a country that lies very far away from here, across the great deserts, to the east. It was not until twenty-seven years after the plague that Johnson reached California. In all that Utah region he reported but three survivors, himself one, and all men. For many years these three men lived and hunted together, until, at last, desperate, fearing that with them the human race would perish utterly from the planet, they headed westward on the possibility of finding women survivors in California. Johnson alone came through the great desert, where his two companions died. He was forty-six years old when he joined us, and he married the fourth daughter of Isadore and Hale, and his eldest son married your aunt, Hare-Lip, who was the third daughter of Vesta and the Chauffeur. Johnson was a strong man, with a will of his own. And it was because of this that he seceded from the Santa Rosans and formed the Utah Tribe at San José. It is a small tribe – there are only nine in it; but, though he is dead, such was his influence and the strength of his breed, that it will grow into a strong tribe and play a leading part in the recivilization of the planet.

'There are only two other tribes that we know of – the Los Angelitos and the Carmelitos. The latter started from one man and woman. He was called Lopez, and he was descended from the ancient Mexicans and was very black. He was a cowherd in the ranges beyond Carmel, and his wife was a maidservant in the great Del Monte Hotel. It was seven years before we first got in touch with the Los Angelitos. They have a good country down there, but it is too warm. I estimate the present population of the world at between three hundred and fifty and four hundred – provided, of course, that there are no scattered little tribes elsewhere in the world. If there be such, we have not heard from them. Since Johnson crossed the desert from Utah, no word nor sign has come from the East or anywhere else. The great world which I knew in my boyhood and early manhood is gone. It has ceased to be. I am the last man who was alive in the days of the plague and who knows the wonders of that far-off time. We, who mastered the planet – its earth, and sea, and sky – and who were as very gods, now live in primitive savagery along the water courses of this California country.

'But we are increasing rapidly – your sister, Hare-Lip, already has four children. We are increasing rapidly and making ready for a new climb toward civilization. In time, pressure of population will compel us to spread out, and a hundred generations from now we may expect our descendants to start across the Sierras, oozing slowly along, generation by generation, over the great continent to the colonization of the East – a new Aryan drift around the world.

'But it will be slow, very slow; we have so far to climb. We fell so hopelessly far. If only one physicist or one chemist had survived! But it was not to be, and we have forgotten everything. The Chauffeur started working in iron. He made the forge which we use to this day. But he was a lazy man, and when he died he took with him all he knew of metals and machinery. What was I to know of such things? I was a classical scholar, not a chemist. The other men who survived were not educated. Only two things did the Chauffeur accomplish – the brewing of strong drink and the growing of tobacco. It was while he was drunk, once, that he killed Vesta. I firmly believe that he killed Vesta in a fit of drunken cruelty though he always maintained that she fell into the lake and was drowned.

'And, my grandsons, let me warn you against the medicine-men. They call themselves *doctors*, travestying what was once a noble profession, but in reality they are medicine-men, devil-devil men, and they make for superstition and darkness. They are cheats and liars. But so debased and degraded are we, that we believe their lies. They, too, will increase in numbers as we increase, and they will strive to rule us. Yet are they liars and charlatans. Look at young Cross-Eyes, posing as a doctor, selling charms against sickness, giving good hunting, exchanging promises of fair weather for good meat and skins, sending the death-stick, performing a thousand abominations. Yet I say to you, that when he says he can do these things, he lies. I, Professor Smith, Professor James Howard Smith, say that he lies. I have told him so to his teeth. Why has he not sent me the death-stick? Because he knows that with me it is without avail. But you, Hare-Lip, so deeply are you sunk in black superstition that did you awake this night and find the death-stick beside you, you would surely die. And you would die, not because of any virtues in the stick, but because you are a savage with the dark and clouded mind of a savage.

'The doctors must be destroyed, and all that was lost must be discovered over again. Wherefore, earnestly, I repeat unto you certain things which you must remember and tell to your children after you. You must tell them that when water is made hot by fire, there resides in it a wonderful thing called steam, which is stronger than ten thousand men and which can do all man's work for him. There are other very useful things. In the lightning flash resides a similarly strong servant of man, which was of old his slave and which some day will be his slave again.

'Quite a different thing is the alphabet. It is what enables me to know the meaning of fine markings, whereas you boys know only rude picture-writing. In that dry cave on Telegraph Hill, where you see me often go when the tribe is down by the sea, I have stored many books. In them is great wisdom. Also, with them, I have placed a key to the alphabet, so that one who knows picture-writing may also know print. Some day men will read again; and then, if no accident has befallen my cave, they will know that Professor James Howard Smith once lived and saved for them the knowledge of the ancients.

'There is another little device that men inevitably will rediscover. It is called gunpowder. It was what enabled us to kill surely and at long distances. Certain things which are found in the ground, when combined in the right proportions, will make this gunpowder. What these things are, I have forgotten, or else I never knew. But I wish I did know. Then would I make powder, and then would I certainly kill Cross-Eyes and rid the land of superstition – '

'After I am man-grown I am going to give Cross-Eyes all the goats, and meat, and skins I can get, so that he'll teach me to be a doctor,' Hoo-Hoo asserted. 'And when I know, I'll make everybody else sit up and take notice. They'll get down in the dirt to me, you bet.'

The old man nodded his head solemnly, and murmured:

'Strange it is to hear the vestiges and remnants of the complicated Aryan speech falling from the lips of a filthy little skin-clad savage. All the world is topsy-turvy. And it has been topsy-turvy ever since the plague.'

'You won't make me sit up,' Hare-Lip boasted to the would-be medicine-man. 'If I paid you for a sending of the death-stick and it didn't work, I'd bust in your head – understand, you Hoo-Hoo, you?'

'I'm going to get Granser to remember this here gunpowder stuff,' Edwin said softly, 'and then I'll have you all on the run. You, Hare-Lip, will do my fighting for me and get my meat for me, and you, Hoo-Hoo, will send the death-stick for me and make everybody afraid. And if I catch Hare-Lip trying to bust your head, Hoo-Hoo, I'll fix him with that same gunpowder. Granser ain't such a fool as you think, and I'm going to listen to him and some day I'll be boss over the whole bunch of you.'

The old man shook his head sadly, and said:

'The gunpowder will come. Nothing can stop it – the same old story over and over. Man will increase, and men will fight. The gunpowder will enable men to kill millions of men, and in this way only, by fire and blood, will a new civilization, in some remote day, be evolved. And of what profit will it be? Just as the old civilization passed, so will the new. It may take fifty thousand years to build, but it will pass. All things pass. Only remain cosmic force and matter, ever in flux, ever acting and reacting and realizing the eternal types – the priest, the soldier, and the king. Out of the mouths of babes comes the wisdom of all the ages. Some will fight, some will rule, some will pray; and all the rest will toil and suffer sore while on their bleeding carcasses is reared again, and yet again, without end, the amazing beauty and surpassing wonder of the civilized state. It were just as well that I destroyed those cave-stored books – whether they remain or perish, all their old truths will be discovered, their old lies lived and handed down. What is the profit – '

Hare-Lip leaped to his feet, giving a quick glance at the pasturing goats and the afternoon sun.

'Gee!' he muttered to Edwin, 'The old geezer gets more long-winded every day. Let's pull for camp.'

While the other two, aided by the dogs, assembled the goats and started them for the trail through the forest, Edwin stayed by the old man and guided him in the same direction. When they reached the old right of way, Edwin stopped suddenly and looked back. Hare-Lip and Hoo-Hoo and the dogs and the goats passed on. Edwin was looking at a small herd of wild horses which had come down on the hard sand. There were at least twenty of them, young colts and yearlings and mares, led by a beautiful stallion which stood in the foam at the edge of the surf, with arched neck and bright wild eyes, sniffing the salt air from off the sea.

'What is it?' Granser queried.

'Horses,' was the answer. 'First time I ever seen 'em on the beach. It's the mountain lions getting thicker and thicker and driving 'em down.'

The low sun shot red shafts of light, fan-shaped, up from a cloud-tumbled horizon. And close at hand, in the white waste of shore-lashed waters, the sea-lions, bellowing their old primeval chant, hauled up out of the sea on the black rocks and fought and loved.

'Come on, Granser,' Edwin prompted. And old man and boy, skin-clad and barbaric, turned and went along the right of way into the forest in the wake of the goats.

Notes

1. Crawley, Richard, Trans [online], *Thucydides: The History of the Peloponnesian War* (London: Spottiswood, 1874), accessed 28 November 2020. Available at: www.gutenberg.org.
2. Finnegan, Rachel, 'Plagues in Classical Literature', *Classics Ireland*, 6 (1999), 23–42 (p. 27).
3. Papagrigorakis, Manolis J., Yapijakis, Christos, and Synodinos, Philippos N., 'Typhoid Fever Epidemic in Ancient Athens', in *Paleomicrobiology: Past Human Infections*, ed. by Raoult, Didier and Drancourt, Michel (New York: Springer Science & Business Media, 2008), pp. 161–73.
4. Holloday, A.J. and Poole, J.C.F. 'Thucydides and the Plague of Athens', *The Classical Quarterly*, 29: 2 (1979), 282–300 (p. 296).
5. Crawley, op. cit.
6. Driver, G.R., 'The Plague of the Philistines (1 Samuel v, 6-vi, 16)', *The Journal of the Royal Asiatic Society of Great Britain and Ireland*, 1 (1950), 50-52. Driver disputes this and argues instead that the plague was dysentery.
7. Procopius [online], *History of the Wars of Justinian*, Trans. Dewey, H.B., Loeb Library of Greek and Roman Classics, 7 vols (Cambridge, MA: Harvard University Press, 1914), accessed 10 January 2020, available at www.wikisource.com (licensed under Creative Commons for commercial and non-commercial use).
8. *The Anglo-Saxon Chronicle* [online], Trans. James Ingram and J.A. Giles, accessed 30 January 2021. Available at: www.gutenberg.org.
9. Madicott, J.R., 'Plague in Seventh-Century England', *Past & Present*, 156: 1 (1997), 7–54.
10. Shrewsbury, J.F.D., 'The Yellow Plague', *Journal of the History of Medicine and Allied Sciences*, 4: 1 (1949), pp. 5–47.
11. Madicott, 37.
12. Sellar, A.M., *An Ecclesiastical History of England: A Revised Translation* (London: George Bell, 1906), v.iii.xxvii.

13. Skene, William F., Trans. *John of Fordun's Chronicle of the Scottish Nation* (Edinburgh: Edmonston and Douglas, 1872), p. 119.
14. Kendall, Elizabeth Kimball, Trans. *Source Book of English History* (New York: MacMillan, 1900), pp. 102–06.
15. Boccaccio, Giovanni [online], *The Decameron*, Trans. James McMullen Rigg, 2 vols (London: A.H. Bullen, 1903), accessed 10 January 2021, available at: wikisource.org.
16. Taken from *Select Poetry, Chiefly Sacred, of the Reign of King James the First*, ed. by Farr, Edward (Cambridge: University Press, 1847).
17. Taken from *The Collected Works of Thomas Nashe*, ed. by Grosart, Alexander B., 6 vols (London: Privately Printed, 1883–84).
18. Taken from *The Works of Daniel Defoe*, ed. by Keltie, John S. (Edinburgh: William P. Nimmo, 1869).
19. Carver, Stephen *The Author who Outsold Dickens: The Life and Work of W.H. Ainsworth* (Barnsley: Pen and Sword, 2020), p. 131.
20. Taken from Ainsworth, William Harrison, *Old Saint Paul's*, 3 vols (London: Cunningham, 1841).
21. Taken from Hood, Thomas, *The Works of Thomas Hood* (London: Ward and Lock, 1899).
22. This extract is taken from Poe, Edgar Allen, *Tales of the Grotesque and Arabesque*, 2 vols (Philadelphia: Lea and Blanchard, 1840).
23. Taken from Poe, Edgar Allen 'The Mask of the Red Death: A Fantasy', *Graham's Magazine*, May (1842), 22–26.
24. This extract is taken from Reynolds, G.W.M., *Faust: A Romance of the Secret Tribunals* (London: John Dicks, 1884).
25. Taken from Shelley, Mary, *The Last Man*, 3 vols (London: Henry Colburn, 1826).
26. Taken from London, Jack, *The Scarlet Plague* (London: Mills and Boon, 1912).